The Good City and
the Good Life

THE

Good City

AND THE

Good Life

DANIEL KEMMIS

A Marc Jaffe Book

HOUGHTON MIFFLIN COMPANY

BOSTON   NEW YORK   1995

For information about permission to reproduce selections from
this book, write to Permissions, Houghton Mifflin Company,
215 Park Avenue South, New York, New York 10003.

For information about this and other Houghton Mifflin
trade and reference books and multimedia products, visit
The Bookstore at Houghton Mifflin on the World Wide Web
at http://www.hmco.com/trade/.

Library of Congress Cataloging-in-Publication Data
Kemmis, Daniel, date.
The good city and the good life / Daniel Kemmis.
p.   cm.
Includes bibliographical references
ISBN 0-395-68630-X
1. Community life. 2. Political culture —
United States.   I. Title.
HM131.K398   1995
307 — dc20   95-19258
CIP

Printed in the United States of America

QUM 10 9 8 7 6 5 4 3 2 1

Book design by Melodie Wertelet

To the good citizens of Missoula . . .

in remembrance, in fellowship,

in faithful expectation

Acknowledgments

Once I let the idea of the good life lay its full claim on my writing, I found myself surrounded by teachers wherever I went.

My colleagues in the work of governing Missoula had long been teaching me, through their dedication to serving the city so remarkably well, how richly textured is the fabric of care upon which the city's excellence depends.

Getting me to the right place at the right time for whatever the next lesson might be has been no easy task, and I cannot imagine having done any of this without the remarkably able assistance of Kate Pope.

Wherever I traveled, people taught me about their cities, sometimes without knowing they were teaching me anything at all. Friends at the National League of Cities, the Kettering Foundation, and the Pew Partnership for Civic Change provided me, among them, with centuries of accumulated wisdom. I especially appreciated conversations with Seattle's former mayor, Charles Royer, and Charleston's mayor, Joseph Riley. Nowhere did such wisdom run deeper than among the folks at the Dallas Institue for Humanities and Culture. Gail Thomas and Robert Sardello in particular fixed my faith on the soul of the city, while to faithful friends and colleagues such as Anita Doyle, Sally Thompson Greiser, Albert Borgmann, Dennis Taylor, Mary Walsh, Geoff Badenoch, and Greg Oliver I owe the knowing of it in my own city.

Because mayoring is full-time work in Missoula, I could only write on weekends. That left my sons with fewer pancake breakfasts than they deserved, and Jeanne with fewer conversations on the deck. Still, no one has taught me more about the subject of this book than my family as we have woven the fabric of our lives always more richly into the life of our city. Beyond that, Abe's editorial help was deeply valuable, and provided an unusual chance for me to share my work with him.

How I could have been lucky enough to bring this book under Marc Jaffe's editorial aegis I will never entirely know, but it is a kind of luck I do not intend to question.

Contents

Foreword

❈

RICHEY WAS THE TOWN nearest our small family farm on the high, dry, windy plains of eastern Montana, which meant that it was in Richey, a metropolis of some six hundred people, that I first experienced anything of town life. A painfully bashful child, I could only with the greatest difficulty survive an introduction to any stranger, while the town seemed endlessly supplied with strangers I must meet. I lived for Friday night, when we could go back home for two long days and three nights of familiar terrain, of cows and horses whose names I already knew, and who seemed content with whatever they already knew of me.

For reasons that remain wrapped in impenetrable paradox, this hopelessly reclusive child had already, by the time he was eight years old, developed a fascination with politics that would dog his steps all his life, through a decade of service in the state legislature, including the intense partisanship of stints as minority leader and Speaker of the House, and then into two terms as the full-time mayor of a city at the other end of Montana from the remote farm of his childhood.

But of course the child, unable to foresee with any clarity how this political career might unfold, had to imagine his own picture of it. Daydreaming is one of the great luxuries of childhood, and the boy, whose life contained no luxuries that might cost money, indulged this free one with considerable abandon.

Beginning around the age of ten or eleven, he developed a habit of concerted daydreaming in the half hour or so before he fell asleep at night. For weeks at a stretch, he would work out and elaborate a story line until all its allure had been exhausted, when he would regretfully leave that story and begin building another. It was here that he lay his emerging political aspirations before himself.

Richey as he barely knew it had little to offer as daydream material, but the larger world supplied a place to begin. He and his classmates had all been born within months of the devastation of Hiroshima, which meant that they were the first of that wave of children who would spend their lives as "baby boomers." Like everyone else in the fifties, these children practiced nuclear attack responses, both the more leisurely parade to the school basement, now stocked as an air raid shelter, and the short-notice dive under their desks, where the young politician never thought about incinerating explosions so much as about the series of past generations of third graders who had all stuck their chewing gum on what was now his ceiling. It was perhaps that experience of huddling down there, giggling at one another's absurdity, that prepared these children and their peers everywhere to respond so powerfully a few years later to a story like *Lord of the Flies*, in which the children find themselves the only ones left, and then have to decide what to make of the situation.

So prepared, it was embarrassingly predictable that this boy's first remembered bedtime story line should be of the aftermath of a nuclear attack survived solely by his classmates and himself. Here they were, then, living in a little city of tents spread out across the familiar terrain of the playground. The rest of the town, including the school itself, was gone, and not an adult remained. The children were completely on their own, and completely in charge.

Here the politician launched his career, and while he may have experimented during the first few nights of his fantasy with authoritarian or at least authoritative methods of governing, he came unexpectedly to a very different image of what his role would be in this city of his peers. None of the others wanted to be politicians, so he had that field to himself. What he found himself doing in his tent, though, was not ruling, not making laws, not exercising any of the kinds of power with which his daytime reading of political biographies had already made him familiar. What he did instead was to listen to those of his classmates who had fallen into disputes, either about personal matters such as who was whose boy- or girlfriend, or about how the town should be organized and operated. He would listen to both sides, and then try to get the disputants to figure out some workable solution to the problem. Just how he helped them find those solutions has never been quite clear to me, but the image of his post-Armageddon politics has never entirely faded from my memory.

Forty years later, working with the Leadership Training Council of the National League of Cities, or with the National Civic League or the Pew Partnership for Civic Change, I have discovered that hundreds of my peers in city halls across the country are experimenting with a kind of politics that begins to look very much like those after-the-bomb imaginings. Only now, in a sense, the plot line has actually fallen into place, as the responsibility for how things will turn out has come squarely to rest on the shoulders of those kids on the playground. The fact that so many local politicians now devote so much energy to learning new techniques of mediation and collaborative problem solving has sometimes made me think that the way that childish daydream unfolded had been in some way predetermined by the entire historical context of the postwar generation.

Our situation had instilled in us a largely unspoken but deeply implanted fear that there may be no future for us at all. Is it not possible that we have always known, in some collectively unconscious foresight, that a world so wounded, so near the mirror of its own annihilation, could only be well inhabited by developing some ways of being together that would differ radically from those forms that had created the crisis that was our world? If we did end up with a world to inhabit, to govern, to pass on, might there not have been a kind of species wisdom that would have told us, however faintly, that the task of carrying life forward could only succeed if we learned to call much more broadly on the human potential of everyone on the playground? From the struggle this generation had to live out between death and despair on the one hand and life and hope on the other, might there not be generated some unexpected ways of affirming the insistent power of life even in the face of death?

Such life-affirming forms are in fact emerging around the globe, with ever greater cogency and force, but they remain obscured by the prevailing political forms of another age. Like some snake shedding its skin, we focus our attention on that which no longer serves us, and undervalue if we notice at all the tender but vital container emerging to replace it.

As one determined from childhood to find in politics an honorable calling, I find myself now compelled to acknowledge that our prevailing politics is steadily dehumanizing us, and that we seem incapable of making it serve us better. Nearly every national election leads a host of commentators to call that particular campaign the most negative, bitter, angry, and ugly anyone can recall. Which election will actually prove to have won that prize remains to be seen, and must remain undetermined until something finally produces a change in the way we do politics. But where will such change come from? "Angry

times . . . breed angry campaigns," a *New York Times* analysis
of the 1994 election concluded. "What is less clear . . . is how
the cycle ever ends."

Perhaps part of the problem is that we have cast politics in
a fundamentally dehumanizing frame, so that no amount of
tinkering with structure (as in term limits or balanced budget
amendments) and no amount of switching polarities (by responding to proclamations that "It's time for a change!") can
make politics feel humanly satisfying. But maybe we need to
loosen the canvas of politics from the frame in which we have
viewed it for so long and try, at least in our imaginations, to
see how it would look in a very different kind of frame. If the
threat of extinction did nothing else, it should have prepared
us for such a reframing, whether in childhood imagination or
in adult practice.

The old frame has been, quite simply, the nation-state. Our
entire political landscape is focused by the national government, and especially by the presidency. We continue to believe,
with an astonishing lack of critical examination, and against
steadily mounting evidence to the contrary, that the nation is
the vehicle by which we must move to a more humane future.
We put most of our politically psychic energy into that enterprise, and we judge how well our democratic culture is faring
by how well the national government functions. Not surprisingly, using that measure of our capacity for self-government,
we become terribly discouraged, bitter, angry, and sullen; we
switch pilots with mounting frenzy, hoping blindly that raw,
undifferentiated "change" will make the framework serve us
better. But this way of framing our politics, while it may still
have some modest capacity to serve us, is certainly not going to
save us, and it will not restore our deeply severed trust in the
very future of life.

If we were to look elsewhere for a frame better suited both

to humankind's challenges and to its profound potential, and for a standard by which to judge the human dimensions of our politics, we might do worse than to repair to the biblical measure "that they might have life and have it more abundantly." It is the deep and varied bounty of life that we dimly but fervently seek to nurture and secure through politics, and it is by this measure that we might judge any framework within which we conduct our human affairs. If we make the abundance of life our focus, we can see that we have already begun to view the human situation in a framework that has everything to do with life and little or nothing to do with nationhood.

Like many another mayor around the world, I have mounted on my office wall an enlarged satellite photograph of my city. Taken from five hundred miles above the earth, the photo displays clearly the folds of the mountains surrounding the Missoula Valley, picturing the city itself clearly enough that children who visit my office can pick out their neighborhood parks and sometimes even their schools and playgrounds. Because the children find this image so fascinating, I often unroll for them a companion picture, which is simply the same shot reproduced at a scale that allows us to see in one glance where Missoula sits "at the hub of the five valleys," a natural pocket of human inhabitation in the midst of a twenty million–plus acre forested ecosystem about which the children are as curious (and often as knowledgeable) as they are about their own city.

Sometimes we move from the aerial photos to a book in which the children can view satellite images of the entire globe, at which point several of them inevitably raise concerns about global warming, the ozone layer, or the loss of animal or plant species. At whatever scale the children and I view these satellite images, we end up speaking both about the earth's phenomenal work of generating life and about the fragility of that creation. Almost without exception, these conversations with young citizens leave me musing about what I have come to experience as the corresponding fragility of the political culture they will inherit to deal with the challenges they so earnestly bring forward to the mayor. And just as inevitably, I then find myself recalling my own youth, my own schoolyard, and my own childhood experience of life's fragility and of its irrepressible promise. I recall, in other words, that little tent city, bravely and hopefully springing up in the face of all that threatens and diminishes life.

Almost every month throughout the late fifties and early sixties, a new crisis erupted somewhere on the globe, bringing the superpowers once again to the brink of confrontation. The Cuban Missile Crisis was the most memorable of these, the one during which the largest number of people allowed themselves to think seriously of the possibility of global destruction. But earlier there had been the U-2 spy plane incident, the Bay of Pigs, and a period of icy tension over Berlin, culminating in President Kennedy's trip to that city in 1963.

Brutally severed by the newly constructed wall, the city had become the symbol of a severed world, and of that world's uncertain capacity to continue sustaining life. Few political utterances in the second half of this century have stirred more hearts more deeply than Kennedy's four brief words of well-coached German: "Ich bin ein Berliner!" Nothing has done more, thirty years later, to restore people's hope that the world might indeed have a future than the restoring of that city to wholeness. Kennedy's claim that we were all citizens of Berlin rang so deeply because it was a way of reminding us that we were all citizens of the world, and all deeply fearful about the world's ongoing capacity to sustain life. Now that the city has been restored we can begin to imagine once again a world rejoined to its future, a people rejoined to its hope, a politics beyond the politics of universal anger and mistrust.

The satellite picture on my wall came from a biology laboratory on the University of Montana campus. The main interest of the scientists who gave it to me is to get the clearest picture they possibly can of the vegetation in our northern reaches of the Rocky Mountains, so that they can better understand how plants and animals establish and maintain among themselves a sustainable ecosystem. The different colors on the map reveal where ponderosa pine resides; where it gives way to larch, where the grasslands of the valley floor reign, and, within all these forms of life, where human habitation predominates.

The photo does not enable us to see individual pine trees, let alone the individual elk or bear cubs that move under them, but we know that in the end, the health of the ecosystem and the well-being of the individuals within it are so mutually interdependent as to be indistinguishable from each other. We cannot see, either, the individual Missoulians carrying on their daily lives within the portion of the ecosystem their city has become. If the photo were taken on election day, we would have no sense of the relative level of their anger, bitterness, or sullenness. But neither would we be able to see the countless small acts of kindness, of hope, of cooperation by which they sustain and nurture the fundamental goodness of the city they call home. It is in those intensely human activities that the revitalization of democratic politics must occur.

And it is there that it is in fact occurring, with a steadily increasing intensity, in city after city around the globe. There, by thousands of small, patient steps, whole cities are learning once again to take responsibility for the lives and the hopes of their children. As cities come to understand that they themselves cannot survive if their children have no hope, the nurturing of hope becomes part of the city's work, and with it the nurturing and rebuilding of trust, without which democracy simply disintegrates.

Obscured by the ground cover of an entirely different kind of politics, the self-generated healing of cities, occurring always at the most intensely human scale, goes on almost unnoticed while we cast about frantically for what might redeem democracy. This book is meant as an invitation to get our feet on the ground, to walk around for a short time under the trees, to pay attention to the ways the earth might be attempting to heal itself and us through the subtle but powerful healing of its living cities.

The Good City and
the Good Life

ONE

The Good Life

The city comes into existence, originating in the bare
needs of life, and continuing in existence for the sake
of a good life. —ARISTOTLE, *Politics*

B Y THE TIME Abe and I get out of the house, onto our
bikes, across the river, and down to the north end of
Higgins Avenue, the bell has already rung and the first exchanges of the Saturday morning Missoula Farmers' Market
have been completed. In fact, there are already a few people
leaving the market as we walk our bikes across the last intersection, into the plaza near the old Northern Pacific depot. I'm
always surprised and just a little annoyed that anyone would
take such a flatly commercial view of the market. They've got
their strawberries — the first of the crop — and now they're
going home. Arriving after the bell rings, I know that I won't
be getting any strawberries, and my flash of annoyance shifts
briefly from the departing shoppers to Abe, until I remind
myself that a teenager can't be expected to wake instanta-
neously after a mere twelve hours' sleep. As for the strawberry
grabbers, I have told myself often enough that it takes all kinds
to make a city, and I'm about to experience the city at its best,
so let them take their strawberries.

A week earlier, I had been asked to help the market celebrate its twentieth anniversary. It had been a special event for

me, not only because the Saturday morning market had become such a pleasant staple of my summer routine, but because one of the founders who was to be honored that morning had been a friend of mine since shortly after my arrival in Missoula, during the market's first summer. She had also been one of the first people to urge me to run for mayor, years before I finally decided to seek the office from which I now had a chance to honor both the market and my old friend. Mavis was to receive a plaque as one of the market's cofounders, but when I arrived at Circle Square that Saturday morning, one of her friends drew me aside, showed me the garland of homegrown flowers she had prepared, and asked if I would crown Mavis after I presented the plaque. I would, and I did, and all the early birds laughed and cheered as the market master rang the bell to begin the market's twenty-first year.

Now, a week later, the festivities are behind us, but I catch a glimpse of Mavis across the square, and remind myself to watch for her as I make my way through the crowd. After twenty years of maturing, the market has become so popular and busy that you can never be sure you'll actually get to talk to someone you've spied at a distance. Knowing from experience how chancy connections can be, Abe and I agree to rendezvous in half an hour beside the nineteenth-century locomotive which recalls the railroading history of this end of Missoula. Then I get in line for the best coffee in town, and Abe heads into the crowd in search of cinnamon rolls. An old friend joins me in the line. His wife scolds him for attending to coffee before cauliflower, but his attitude is much like mine: the market is more than produce and commodity exchange. We'll visit while we wait in line for our coffee, then sit and listen to the live brass quintet while we drink it, visit some more, and greet a few friends. Then it will be time enough to start buying vegetables.

The sellers at our market are about evenly balanced between western Montana old-timers and Hmong immigrants who have been our neighbors now since shortly after the market was launched. The market experienced a crisis a few years ago when the Hmong began arriving at the plaza long before the opening bell and claiming all the prize spots. To some, they were simply being as aggressive as any new culture might well be in carving out a foothold in a strange land, but from the perspective of many of the old-time native sellers (who had no intention of getting up that early on Saturday morning) they were being altogether too aggressive. I remember Mavis and my former law partner, Joan Jonkel, calling me as their representative on the city council and a tireless (if not tiresome) advocate of consensus decisions, to ask what in the world they were supposed to do about this conundrum. Their beloved market was in danger of coming apart at the seams, and what was worst for my two liberal friends was the fear that if it did, it would be over an issue in which an eager observer could readily see or imagine racist overtones.

I had little advice to offer at the time except to keep talking and to talk straight about everything, including the concern about racism and about the market. Guided far more by their own common sense and passion than by my advice, Joan and Mavis and the Hmong leaders worked out a space assignment policy which most of us never knew about except indirectly, as this morning Abe would know where the Mammyth Bakery cinnamon rolls would be and I would know where Neng Moua and his family would be offering the most generous portion of the season's first green beans.

I would know, too, that at the end of the block-long arcade — the brick-lined avenue that had once been Railroad Street — I would find the booth of the region's most prominent organic farmers, Lifeline Produce. I'd reserve a number of purchases until I made my way to Lifeline. Broccoli, for example, I knew from my own gardening experience, was subject in this climate to fierce attacks of cabbage moths and their offspring, "cabbage loopers." When the translucent green worms started eating silver dollar–size holes in your broccoli leaves, the temptation to spray grew almost unbearable — or even a shade beyond almost. But Steve and Lucy, I knew to a certainty, had not sprayed chemicals on their broccoli.

I'd known Lucy since the seventies, when she came to Missoula as an environmental studies graduate student at the University of Montana, and I, as a state legislator, had been asked to address the new recruits. A couple of years later, as she approached the culmination of her master's degree program, Lucy came to Helena to testify on environmental issues at the state legislature, and I started to ask what she and her colleagues were going to do once they graduated. Lucy didn't know in March and three months later still didn't know, and it began to seem that in her case my description of the environmental studies program as bringing bright, committed people to Missoula from all over the country and turning them into Montanans wasn't going to work. Then, just when I had reconciled myself to the idea that Lucy was going back to her grandmother's home in Texas, she came to my law office to tell me about a new organic farm in the Bitterroot Valley south of Missoula. It sounded awfully starry-eyed and chancy to me, but now this morning, buying broccoli from Lucy and her tall, sun-browned husband whom she'd met and married on the farm seven years ago, I could only say under my breath, "You knew best, Lucy!"

At the Lifeline booth, as at every other stop I make on my tour under the rapidly warming July sun, I'm almost certain to find my purchases mixed with talk as friends, acquaintances, or, in the case of the mayor, utter strangers, inject conversation into the midst of the broccoli, green beans, and fresh-baked bread. During the course of the market's two hours, the conversations will run a gamut from Little League to potholes to events in Eastern Europe, but what I have come to be as attentive to are the unspoken conversations. As Steve weighs my broccoli and Lucy counts out my change, the whole history of their farm and of our friendship is part and parcel of what we exchange. When I do come across Mavis and she launches into one of her "I've got a bone to pick with you, Daniel" speeches, all those years of her urging me to run for mayor lie behind the fierce but friendly challenge in her eyes. Moving through the market, back toward the spot where I'm to meet Abe, I see in dozens of conversations around me an interweaving of these life stories, and I find delight and security in realizing once again that this fabric is Missoula, my home, my city.

Just as I catch sight of Abe eating his cinnamon roll and balancing mine on his knees where he sits next to the plaza's ancient locomotive, I am intercepted by another old friend, a retired university professor whose fine-tuned insights I have treasured since I studied German with her as a graduate student during my first years in Missoula. Smiling as she approaches me, she sums up everything I have been thinking, as with a sweep of her hand, taking in the market at large, she asks in her soft German accent, "Isn't this civilized?"

Finally, the sum of all the unspoken conversations from one end of the market plaza to the other comes down to an acknowledgment that this is pretty much what we all had in mind. The twenty-year tradition of celebrating the coming to fruition of the valley's gardens has finally itself ripened into a second-order coming to fruition. Increasingly now at Farmers' Market, Missoulians celebrate the maturing of their own life together. When Gertrud refers to the market as civilized, she uses a term I have heard more than once in this setting. It is not a word which ever comes easily or lightly. The tone with which it is spoken always seems to recognize that this is a word hallowed by its application to places and times of proven excellence. But in calling the market civilized, its celebrants acknowledge that the good life is not just some abstraction mummified in history books or perhaps occurring half a world away, but that it is richly if only roughly present here and now, in this plaza, on this July morning.

I know that one of the reasons I enjoy the Farmers' Market is because it represents for me the best of the city in microcosm. If I can understand the market, I will know more about my city. And if I can see what Gertrud means when she calls the market civilized, I might learn something about the city's own capacity to sustain that word, and thus to nurture both the good life and the healing of our political culture.

Why would anyone even imagine that something like the Farmers' Market could play a role in mending a suffering democracy? Fixated as we are on "important" state and national issues such as term limits, campaign finance reform, crime, health care, and welfare reform, this suggestion seems at first to be merely frivolous. But, in fact, none of the other paths to reform on which people expend so much energy will reverse the decline of democracy, and none of the policies that we enact to deal with pressing problems such as poverty, racism, environmental damage, and drug and alcohol abuse will do any more than slow the worsening of these evils until we begin to understand the political importance of events like the Farmers' Market. No amount of reforming institutions that are widely and rightly perceived to be beyond human scale will heal our political culture until we begin to pay attention once again to democracy as a human enterprise. Without healing the human base of politics, we will not restore democracy itself. One thing alone will give us the capacity to heal our politics and to confront the problems and opportunities that politics must address. That one thing is a deeply renewed human experience of citizenship.

To redeem the democratic potential of citizenship, we need to take an entirely fresh look at its essential features. One of those, surprisingly, is citizenship's intimate connection to the city, from which both its name and its fundamental human significance derive. What makes a city civilized is something that is also absolutely fundamental to citizenship: in both instances, the basic feature is the human element. In the case of citizenship, this facet will make its claim most clearly if we allow it to appear, not where we might expect to find it, in governmental institutions, or in theories or documents, but in the most unassumingly human settings. This book will take us to many such settings in many parts of the city. For the remainder of this chapter, we will focus on how a few city markets, both in their evolution and in the way people relate to them, might have something hopeful to tell us about the human roots of democracy. It will take most of this book to explain why I believe that Gertrud's way of standing and speaking when she asks if the market isn't civilized are precisely the stance and the voice of the truly democratic citizen. It will be a start in that direction, and a start toward explaining what it is that must be healed, if we move from Gertrud to a very different stance and voice — one all too familiar within our prevailing political culture.

The Missoula Area Conferencing System was an early version of a computer network that served, among other functions, as a kind of town hall where a variety of citizens, elected officials, and local government employees exchanged news and views about a broad range of issues. The exchanges were informal and open, often educational, and occasionally heated.

One day, shortly after the city's semiannual tax statements appeared in mailboxes throughout Missoula, one of the network's participants entered an inquiry into the system concerning the increase in her taxes. This very polite request triggered a passionate response from a fellow named Jerry. I have since learned that computer bulletin boards often evoke fully uninhibited, blindly passionate entries, and that this kind of response has earned the title "flaming." Jerry was flaming, which is to say that, like many others who address themselves to public issues, he was literally beside himself. Here is the unedited text of Jerry's message:

> you are not alone in your frustrations with the city. all thay want is more tax money so thay can do less. thay can't take care of what thay have now what can we look forward to when thay inlarge the city, more potholes, more taxes. thay (the people in power of the city, these are not the taxpayers) will vote in a rase for themselfs when the #$%& is about to hit the fan.

The lack of literary refinement in Jerry's treatise is purely incidental; in fact, one of the strengths of this electronic forum is that many people who would not otherwise feel comfortable about putting their political sentiments in writing are for some reason less inhibited in this medium. The system then in use in Missoula also carried with it a nicely leveling effect, in that it offered only the crudest of editing tools, so that participants were always sending out plenty of misspelled words. Still, there is something remarkable about Jerry's consistent misspelling of "they." His rendering it as "thay" captures as the correct spelling never could the forbidding otherness which Jerry, like so many others, perceive as the essence of the political system.

"Thay" in their self-seeking perfidy are to blame for it all. And to whom are "thay" contrasted? Why, to "the taxpayers," of course. Now to Jerry's credit, let it be understood that he speaks for vast segments of the populace, both in his inadvertently eloquent rendering of the overwhelming otherness of "thay" and in his naming of all those whom "thay" victimize as "the taxpayers." But it is time that we looked this hard reality in the face: the growing magnitude of the numbers for whom Jerry speaks so plainly is proof that all our smug pride in our "democratic" form of government is an increasingly untenable delusion.

People who customarily refer to themselves as taxpayers are not even remotely related to democratic citizens. Yet this is precisely the word that now regularly holds the place which in a true democracy would be occupied by "citizens." Taxpayers bear a dual relationship to government, neither half of which has anything at all to do with democracy. Taxpayers pay tribute to the government, and they receive services from it. So does every subject of a totalitarian regime. What taxpayers do not do, and what people who call themselves taxpayers have long since stopped even imagining themselves doing, is governing. In a democracy, by the very meaning of the word, the people govern — they create among themselves the conditions of their lives. But in our political culture, "thay" govern, victimizing "the taxpayers" and delivering a uniformly unsatisfactory level of services, not only because of their incredible ineptitude, but because, as Jerry and so many others are darkly convinced, "thay" are draining "the taxpayers'" tribute into their own pockets.

Given the ever worsening dysfunction in the political system at the federal and often at the state level, this sullen attitude is in a large sense entirely justified. Increasingly we seem to be governed at all the "important" levels, where we have learned to judge democracy, by governments that appear to be bought and sold by special interests through PAC contributions, gridlocked by unbending partisanship, unable to solve any major problems, adept only at creating vast new pockets of indebtedness. In the face of such a gigantic failure of democracy, the language that Jerry applies to all politics is not in the least surprising. But perhaps nothing in this scene tells us more about the decline of democratic culture than the lack of any lived, human connection to the concept or practice of citizenship.

It would never have occurred to Jerry to use the word "citizen" instead of "taxpayer." In this he is fully representative of our prevailing political culture. If we do use the word "citizen," it is almost certain either to be part of the phrase "concerned citizen" (as if citizenship were essentially a form of anxiety) or part of the hopelessly confused phrase "private citizen" — the civic equivalent of dry water. Standing by itself, which it rarely does, the word "citizen" evokes all the weariness and unhappiness we associate with public life, so that most of us would not readily, let alone enthusiastically, call ourselves "citizens." But this is only a confirmation of the fact that this word and indeed all of public speech and public life have been so thinned and diluted that we cannot connect them with anything truly vibrant and sustaining.

It would do no good at all simply to insist that we start calling ourselves "citizens" instead of "taxpayers," unless citizenship was already being experienced as something important, worthwhile, and humanly satisfying. People do in fact have an experience of citizenship which is often satisfying, but it does not go by the name of citizenship and is therefore not understood as a political experience, let alone as having any potential to revitalize democracy.

The place to begin, then, is with the experience of citizenship rather than with the word. The opening sketch of the Farmers' Market is one possible description of that experience. I believe that the way people carry themselves at the Farmers' Market is essentially the way of citizens, and that their referring to the market as civilized is an implicit recognition of this fact. Here we stand, then, upon the simple, sustaining, human ground of what might become a living democracy. But to understand how that might be so, we have to ask what this (or any other) market has to do with citizenship or with civilization. We may come to the answer most easily if we first ask what the market has to do with the city, for it is in the city that both citizenship and civilization have their living roots.

We know that most cities through most of history have grown up around markets. We know that people needed gathering places in order to exchange material surplus for deficiency, but also to exchange news, stories, joy, and grief. Through the centuries, cities have continued to be centered around this gathering role, a gathering that enables people to come away from the market more whole than when they arrived. Here at the Farmers' Market, trading surplus for deficiency in a thousand different ways, people are rounding themselves out in the simplest and most satisfying of human terms. Here the ancient work of the city goes on in a refined and satisfying way, evident on the faces and in the gestures of almost everyone I see around me in this plaza.

When Gertrud calls the market "civilized," she alludes to this refinement and this pervasive sense of satisfaction. But the word also recalls the history and the human significance of cities themselves. "Civil" originally meant simply "of the city." Civility was what it took to live next to one another, as cities, by definition, require people to do. But if civility is a requisite for cities to exist at all, civilization goes a stage beyond this. Civilization is not only a city that works by allowing people to live near one another, but a good city — one that enables its inhabitants to live good lives together.

Over the last few years, more and more cities around the world have begun to examine themselves in terms of "livability." Cities now earnestly compete with one another for distinction in this category. In this, we see an attentiveness to the essential human purpose of cities. As we look more closely at how livability is being seriously pursued by cities, one feature will emerge that none of our accustomed ways of thinking about politics or government can have prepared us for. Those traditional constructs have led us to think of political entities exclusively as tools that we deploy for human ends. Nations, states, and cities are, we think, just such tools. Nations and states may indeed be such instruments, and may be able to fulfill their potential by being thought of in that way. But no city that is seen simply as a tool will ever come to be called livable, let alone civilized. The reason is that the city itself is alive, and it is in its own fullness of life that it has the capacity to become humanly livable and humanly fulfilling. If the story of the Farmers' Market is to reveal any fruitful clues about healing our politics, we need to understand how the rounding off, the simple search for a little greater wholeness that the market represents, is reflected in the greater life of the city as a political institution. This fundamental connection between human wholeness and livability and the wholeness and life of the city are all contained in Gertrud's choice of the word "civilized."

When I think of Gertrud's experience growing up in Germany, I try to imagine which features of the cities she knew might be reflected and recalled for her here at Missoula's Farmers' Market. What comes to mind is a description of the good city put forward by a group of architects, led by Christopher Alexander:

> When we look at the most beautiful towns and cities of the past, we are always impressed by a feeling that they are somehow organic. . . . Each of these towns grew as a whole, under its own laws of wholeness . . . and we can feel this wholeness, not only at the largest scale, but in every detail: in the restaurants, in the sidewalks, in the houses, shops, markets, roads, parks, gardens and walls. Even in the balconies and ornaments.[1]

What is so refreshing about Alexander's approach is that he speaks of this wholeness in incremental terms that bring it within human reach. Certainly if we look around any of our large cities today, the picture of wholeness that Alexander shows us seems remote, and if we imagine trying to bring anything like it about by a grand act of will, we must feel immediately defeated. Even here in Missoula, a modest city of some sixty thousand people, any dream of achieving some comprehensive sense of wholeness in the city at large that might mirror what I see around me here at the market would leave me or any of my neighbors in despair.

But Alexander's approach is to remind us of the connection between healing and wholeness, arguing that we have countless opportunities to take small healing steps to move the city in the direction of wholeness. "Every increment of construction," he writes, "must be made in such a way as to heal the city."[2] While the ultimate objective is to realize the wholeness of the city itself, each act of healing has the potential to create smaller pockets of wholeness. According to Alexander, "Every new act of construction has just one basic obligation: it must create a continuous structure of wholes around itself."[3]

These architectural insights about the organic nature of the good city, and about wholeness and healing, carry the promise of a much broader healing than Alexander imagines. Our efforts to address such profound problems as poverty, racism, drug and alcohol abuse, and teenage murders and suicides will continue to fail until we recognize, as Alexander has done, the central importance of wholeness, healing, and health as touchstones of the good city. Those problems can only be solved by a healthy, effective polity. Yet the epidemic dysfunctions in the body politic that Jerry exemplifies — the alienation, despair, and cynicism that are literally destroying democracy — cannot be healed except by nurturing the deeply human aspiration toward health and wholeness. Only citizenship can save politics, and only relatively whole people are capable of reclaiming the human meaning of citizenship from the rubble of a political culture inhabited largely by sullen "taxpayers." Yet there is every reason to believe that the wholeness of the city and of its citizens are utterly dependent upon each other — that neither is possible without the other. This circularity must not be taken as one more excuse for despair. Rather, it should encourage us to bring change within human reach by broadening Alexander's step-at-a-time approach from the physical city to the political culture that is the city's larger self.

Alexander is an architect, and therefore he thinks of healing in terms of building. But important as the physical body of the city is, it alone cannot make the city healthy. The work of healing the city, and with it of healing our political culture, must be carried out not just upon the city's body, but within its heart and soul and mind as well. Yet building is a good place to begin, in part because it can help us to understand the vital relationships among civilization, citizenship, and the good city.

The work of healing the city is civilizing work, which is to say that it creates at one and the same time a better city and better citizens. Recent events in Baltimore illustrate this civilizing process. Baltimore is a city with a newly discovered sense of direction and hope, at the core of which seems to lie a significant revival of citizenship. Inseparable from that revival has been just the kind of healing construction that Alexander describes. Most notable has been the exceptional reclaiming of the waterfront area known as the Inner Harbor, where urban blight has been replaced by a bustling market center next to one of the nation's finest new aquariums. Baltimoreans are so proud of this achievement that they have begun talking about taking the civic energy that could restore a waterfront and using it to restore other, less physical elements of the city. Baltimore may in fact be able to make real its new motto as "The City that Reads," or to make some serious inroads into poverty, racism, and drug abuse, and if it does, it will be in no small part because of the pride and hope that have come from creating good places like the Inner Harbor. It will be because, in Tony Hiss's words, a number of Baltimore citizens

> have hooked together in their heads the downtown story and the waterfront story and the old Federal Hill story with the Hampstead Hill story, which has also been handed down in Baltimore families and taught in Baltimore classrooms, and what they say is that the city has now done enough preliminary work to make it possible to think about banding together to rebuild an entire city all at once.[4]

What is so easy to overlook in this picture is that it is not just successes in the abstract that might produce this greater result, but rather that Baltimore and its citizens have succeeded in creating a number of strong, good places that sustain and nurture citizenship itself. It is precisely the healing of places

— the creation of new structures of wholeness — and the remembrance of the stories of what it took to do this that gives citizens a place to stand, a place to look back in memory and forward in anticipation. Now, because of this civilizing work, as Hiss puts it, "There are lasting places in the city that . . . anchor understandings of what it means to be a Baltimorean."[5]

This is the essence of citizenship in its ancient meaning. Forget for a moment all the weariness that our decaying political culture has encrusted about the word "citizen," and remember that a citizen, in the most basic sense, is simply a city dweller, one whose life is shaped and given identity by the city much as a lion is shaped by and takes its identity from the jungle. A citizen is a denizen of the city: a city-zen. Before we try to make the citizen politically effective, we should understand as fully as possible the more basic human connection between the city and the city-zen. Fundamental to that relationship is the role of those key places that "anchor understandings of what it means to be a Baltimorean" — or a Missoulian or a New Yorker. Tony Hiss's description of one such place (the reading room of Baltimore's Peabody Library) captures the way in which a city might give roots to citizenship:

> The light flooding in through the skylight changes from moment to moment, picking out different colors — gray, buff, gilt — in the columns over your head, and as you sit at one of a number of small desks off the central court, knowledge seems so abundantly available that you feel almost the same kind of gratitude you feel when you stoop to drink from a public fountain: The city doesn't want me to go thirsty.[6]

People who experience the city as sustaining and nurturing them in this way are well on the way to citizenship. Their next step, if given the chance, will often be to seek ways to sustain, nurture, or heal the city. Thus the pattern of healing begins to reinforce itself. Seattle illustrates this civilizing process. In the late 1960s, Seattle's Pike Place Market stood on the verge of obliteration by urban renewal. From a strictly economic vantage, Pike Place's old-fashioned mix of stalls, shops, nooks, and crannies seemed a less than optimal use of an important urban space near Seattle's waterfront. Then, in 1971, a group of citizens who found that they could not imagine Seattle without Pike Place Market organized "Friends of the Market." The group drafted and succeeded in enacting a ballot initiative to preserve and enhance Pike Place. Today, the market is flourishing, while Seattle is recognized as one of America's most livable cities. Among other accomplishments, it has sought and attained a reputation as one of the best cities for young people in the country.

We have come to think of public policy in such segmented, bureaucratic terms that we expect the preservation of Pike Place Market and Seattle's relationship to youth to be entirely separate issues. Recognizing that they are not is an important step toward the healing of our political culture. Making connections among elements of the city that our bureaucratizing methods have severed from one another is crucial to the healing of the city and its citizens. As Jane Jacobs explains, city problems "are all problems which involve dealing simultaneously with a sizable number of factors which are interrelated into an organic whole."[7] Again, architecture offers an illustration of this healing work.

At the same time that Pike Place Market was threatened with extinction, many other old and charming facets of Seattle's downtown were obliterated by the construction of Interstate 5 along the eastern border of the central business district. The same citizen activism that had come to the market's rescue also went to work to heal the damage done by the freeway. Freeway Park was created to soften traffic noise and reestablish severed pedestrian routes. It also provided the impetus for the construction of a convention center in the midst of downtown Seattle, straddling the freeway. Here is how one observer describes the healing work of these projects:

> The transparency of the convention center, and the continuation of colors and materials from outside to inside (the same type of board-formed concrete that appears in Freeway Park also appears inside the building), were meant to suggest to pedestrians that the convention center is as much a part of the public pathway as the park, and as much a part of repairing the damage done by the freeway. [8]

What difference, we are inclined to ask, does it make what the concrete looks like? How can we afford to worry about such trifles when dozens of crack babies are being born every month, some of them probably living within blocks of this freeway? But until our drug policies are as continuous with the rest of the urban fabric as the convention center is with the park, the healing of our great social problems will continue to be what it is now: a worsening failure. Poverty, homelessness, racism, drug addiction, and teenage murders and suicides obviously cry out for an act of healing; so do dysfunctions in the body politic such as alienation, despair, and cynicism. But none of these symptoms can be effectively treated in isolation from the rest, because each dysfunction is itself essentially a reflection of a loss of wholeness. Jane Jacobs is blunt in her criticism of our doomed efforts to isolate and treat any single urban problem:

There is no use wishing it were a simpler problem, because in real life it is not a simpler problem. No matter what you try to do to it, a city park *behaves* like a problem in organized complexity, and that is what it is. The same is true of all other parts or features of cities. Although the interrelations of their many factors are complex, there is nothing accidental or irrational about the ways in which these factors affect each other.[9]

It is for this reason that each act of healing must be understood as an effort to achieve the city's wholeness. And conversely, it is only in its wholeness that the city or any part of it can be healed.

How the wholeness of the city and the healing of a political culture might relate to one another will require a book in the telling. In the chapters that follow, I will explore a number of dimensions of this connection, hoping finally to paint a useful picture of the politically transformative power of the good city. In the meantime, I may as well acknowledge a danger in this approach.

Healing, health, and wholeness are, I am convinced, useful ways of understanding how public life or politics might be revitalized. But no matter how powerful a concept we apply to politics, it is only a concept until it is lived. In some sense this is so true that it hardly bears noting, but when we are speaking of cities, this truth needs attention. For the great thing about cities is that they do, in fact, live. Because of this, no abstraction (including health or wholeness) can ever capture what the city is all about. Only the city itself can do that. As Jane Jacobs says, "City processes in real life are too complex to be routine, too particularized for application as abstractions."[10]

This is important because abstraction has become one of the

great evils of public life, one of the chief ways we tear apart the wholeness of life. Abstraction occurs when we attempt to "abstract" general principles from particular situations and then apply the abstracted principle to every particular situation. Our heavy emphasis on individual rights, to the neglect of a corresponding notion of civic responsibilities, is an example of how abstraction seriously weakens our political culture. Whereas a lived sense of responsibility necessarily grows out of and expresses itself through real relationships among real people, the concept of rights is by its nature abstracted from the particular; this is precisely what we mean when we speak of "a government of laws, not men." No one would deny that the resort to such abstraction has been of vital importance in the struggle against tyranny and oppression. Still, the growing discontent over the protection afforded criminals, or over what many people perceive as the insidious effects of so much of our discrimination law, is a natural human rejection of such thoroughgoing abstraction. Federal environmental laws that are applied to localities regardless of varying local conditions are another example of how our overemphasis on the abstract and the universal has led to serious alienation from public life.

The effects range from the annoying to the bizarre, and sometimes to the maddening. Under the Safe Drinking Water Act, any community sitting atop what federal law calls a "sole source aquifer" must chlorinate its drinking water. Missoula is so situated, yet except in very isolated instances, has never had reason to believe that there is anything dangerous in its water from which chlorine would actually protect its inhabitants. But the federal taste of chlorine is now in every glass of water we draw, and water which was once sweet and refreshing is now avoided by many people for the sake of some public good which none of us have yet managed to understand. As a result, the city is not quite as good a city as it might be; the life of its citizens is not quite as good a life; and, worst of all, our political culture, through which alone we can improve that life or that city, has been incrementally weakened by this flight from the particularity of "organized complexity" to the abstractness of extrinsic solutions.

Abstraction's evil twin in this work is distraction. From drugs and alcohol to TV and workaholism, we are increasingly a society that fulfills T. S. Eliot's description of a people "distracted from distraction by distraction." There is hardly a public menace we can name that is not in some sense caused by one or another of the million ways in which our society teaches and enables us to abstract and distract ourselves — to escape in one way or another from the concrete presence of the here and now.

Cities do their share of distracting, of course. Part of the life of every city is to distract us, and some cities (Las Vegas is my favorite example) seem to have no other reason to exist. But it is not by virtue of this that any city has ever been or might ever be called "civilized." What makes a city a good city is not its capacity to distract, but the way in which it creates presence. Like the "organized complexity" of the city, the concept of presence is richly multidimensional. It is, first of all, a facet of time: the present is that which lies between past and future. Already presence is relational in these terms: we have no way of knowing what we might mean by the present except in relation to past and future. But presence is much more deeply relational than this. If we speak of someone or something being present, we can only mean "present in relationship to something else," and what we really mean then is that they are both temporally and spatially present: they occupy the same "here" and the same "now." Yet even this is only a kind of abstract presence. The concept of presence holds a human significance because we mean by it a way in which beings attentively occupy a common time and place. This presence the good city creates not incidentally, but at the very heart of its excellence.

The gathering function of the marketplace was from the beginning a way of marking off a recognizable here and now within which people and goods could reliably be made present to one another in the dual sense of spatial and temporal presence. Still today, the good city does nothing more important than make it possible for humans to be fully present — to themselves, to one another, and to their surroundings. Such presence is the precise opposite of the distractedness — the being beside oneself — that is so prevalent in our political culture.

The capacity to be present may simply be another feature of health and wholeness. But I am more and more convinced that it is a political value of the highest order, and that citizenship is not conceivable apart from the kind of presence which it is the chief work of the city to create. That this work is subtle and often unassuming should not blind us to its transformative power.

If we were to walk together a few blocks south from the plaza that the Missoula Farmers' Market occupies, we would come to the source of the fine coffee for which my friend and I had stood in line. Butterfly Herbs is downtown Missoula's oldest coffee shop, the place where most of this chapter was written, and the site of a simple, commonplace, but somehow striking tableau which I remember as "the woman at the door."

The coffee shop portion of Butterfly Herbs occupies the back one-third of a long, narrow building which fronts on Higgins Avenue, one of downtown Missoula's main thoroughfares. The high walls at the front of the store carry a vast selection of bulk coffee and tea, as well as some fine pottery, jewelry, and locally produced greeting cards. The store's entrance, recessed behind captivating display cases, provides a passage from street to store and back again through a heavy oaken door which in turn is framed by fine-cut and stained-glass side windows.

One day, shortly after the Farmers' Market birthday, I headed for this door following an hour's writing in the coffee shop. A woman approached the door ahead of me. I was walking briskly, but she moved unhurriedly, taking in her surroundings, examining the wall and window displays as she neared the door. As I drew closer, I could sense her becoming aware of me, and when she reached the door, she pulled it open and held it for me. Walking past her into the recessed alcove off the sidewalk, I tried to grasp what it was about her that so commanded my attention. She struck me as being remarkably self-contained, and yet in no pejorative sense self-centered. Her acknowledgment of me was full and free, and seemed merely an extension of her response to everything around her. The sights, the smells, the music in the store were all incorporated and reflected in her demeanor. The heavy old door itself, and finally, as I passed by her, the sidewalk to which she herself would soon emerge — all were held in dynamic balance by the way she stood poised between the interior of the building and the Missoula street scene beyond.

Since that day, I have often recalled the woman at the door, trying to get to the bottom of the lesson this simple tableau seemed to be teaching about politics. I have not been able to shake off the intuition that if all or even most of my constituents were more like the woman at the door, Missoula would be as well taken care of and its future would be as promising as we could humanly hope for. The contrast between this woman's demeanor and the grinding sullenness of Jerry and his kind lies at the core of both the crisis and the promise in our political culture. I have said that Jerry was beside himself, and have implied that all who wave flags in celebration of our "democracy" while whining about how "thay" victimize "the taxpayers" are in fact beside themselves in a way that threatens democracy far more severely than any conveniently external enemy. But the woman at the door was not beside herself. I am convinced that what accounts for her remarkable presence will prove to be the only sound foundation of democratic citizenship.

Kurt Schmoke, the mayor of Baltimore, has spoken of his vision of Baltimore by the year 2020 having become "a city in grace." Without pretending to know all the subtleties that may be comprehended in Mayor Schmoke's use of this phrase, it seems that a city in grace would necessarily be one in which increasing numbers of Jerrys had been converted into something much more like the woman at the door. Grace is exactly what caught my attention at the door of Butterfly Herbs, and it is just the lack of grace that is so disturbing in Jerry's diatribe, and (far more importantly) in our political culture at large.

The idea of a city in grace is appealing for two seemingly unrelated reasons. First, it answers to a deep longing for a spiritual dimension in public life. In our prevailing political culture, this longing produces one of two results. The first is alienation from public life because it does not fulfill this spiritual need. People do not like politics, or public life in general, because it does not engage their highest or deepest instincts. So they either abandon citizenship altogether, or they import into politics a narrow, essentially mean-spirited religiosity that in fact only worsens the prevailing gracelessness of public life, thus driving new multitudes into alienation. This has been all too much the legacy of the New Right, just as alienation from an inhumanly secularized public life has been the legacy of liberalism. Against this background, Mayor Schmoke's explicit commitment to nurturing some form of grace in public life comes as a rare flash of both spiritual and political wisdom.

But Mayor Schmoke's vision is appealing for a second, equally compelling reason. Put simply, his dream seems to be (if only barely) within human reach. In its concreteness lies its hope. That concreteness is intimately connected to the nature of the political entity of which he speaks. A city in grace, while scarcely imaginable, could actually occur because a city is a living organism, and therefore capable of something we might call grace. We can imagine governors or presidents borrowing Mayor Schmoke's rhetoric and speaking in similar terms of the political entities they govern. But states and nation-states are abstractions to which we cannot easily apply any of the key concepts discussed here: not wholeness, not presence, not grace, and therefore not, I will argue, civilization or citizenship. If we are serious about reclaiming politics, we must give up the bankrupt delusion that a humanly engaging politics can be created where wholeness, presence, or grace are strangers. If the idea of "a city in grace" is to be more than a ringing sound bite, then we have to give full weight to both of its nouns. We need to ask what grace and city might have to do with each other.

Grace is such a prolific concept that no single understanding can exhaust its meaning. But surely some part of grace has to do with a manner of acting in the world that is strikingly appropriate to the time and place. Think of an elegant dive from the high board, or a perfect double play. Such acts are supremely human; they only occur when we bring our very best human traits to bear upon the situation at hand. But such moments always evoke as well an unmistakable element of givenness, of something at least in part beyond our control. What is graceful is, we sense, given to us, as the Baltimorean feels graced when inside the library reading room. The woman at the door was not so gracefully present simply of her own account; rather, she occupied a time and a place that had been given to her. To a substantial extent, the city created that dual presence of time and place, of story and of location, which she so gracefully occupied. Indeed, simply by referring to "the woman at the door," I have all along placed her in this most urban of settings: a passageway from shop to street. All the sights, sounds, smells, and other people of whom she was so palpably aware were city sights and sounds and people. It is in occupying this city-provided presence that she takes on the guise of the city-being, the "city-zen." She captured my attention because of some graceful combination of presence and wholeness. But they were not simply her presence or her wholeness; instead, she occupied and sanctified the presence and the wholeness of the city itself.

It was in part for this kind of sustaining presence, I realize now, that I brought Abe out this morning and sent him into the crowd on his own. And it is this, roughly, that I choose to believe Gertrud meant when she gestured to the market and asked, "Isn't this civilized?" Yes, civilized is the word: presence and wholeness in the never-ending process of becoming, building upon themselves by civilizing (making present and whole) both those who dwell here and the story and place they inhabit. This is the work of the good city. Settling down beside Abe, taking on the sticky challenge of the cinnamon roll he has saved for me, I ask him to describe some of his encounters at the market. First, he looks me full in the face and declares, "Well, I got some strawberries."

"You're kidding!"

Slowly, he unzips his backpack, reaches in, and gingerly lifts out two baby strawberry plants. "Next year," he says, "we won't have to worry about getting here when the bell rings." Next year, I think, we'll have one more story to tell.

A Place to Come Together

What Plato never suspected, apparently, was that the Athens of Solon and Themistocles was itself a greater school than any imaginary commonwealth he was capable of creating in his mind. It was the city itself that had formed and transformed these [Athenians], not alone in a special school or academy, but in every activity, every public duty, in every meeting place and encounter. — LEWIS MUMFORD, *The City in History*

M Y ASSIGNMENT WAS TO TEACH thirty high school juniors about city government. I had already concluded, while still roaming the wide corridors of Sentinel High School searching for room 250, that I would fail. The din around me, the abandon of legs, arms, mouths, and hair, could not possibly transform itself in the next six minutes into a life form receptive to learning about local government. It was May, it was hopeless, and here, for good or ill, was room 250.

As Mr. Stearns's brief introduction approached the event for which I was doing time this morning — my election as mayor — and as the studiously unimpressed faces of my audience obliterated any lingering hope that anyone here might want to learn about city government, especially from the mayor, my rising desperation began formulating a plan of escape. "There is no point in trying to understand city government," I began, and their faces told me they were with me so far, "unless we understand why cities exist at all." I had no idea where this was leading, but it could hardly be worse than the alternative, and it did seem that the facts I had come to impart about city government would be marginally more likely to stick someplace if that place had first become convinced that cities themselves served any human (or still better, adolescent) purpose.

The students soon proved themselves surprisingly adept at discovering and describing the human roots of a city. This may have been the result of the approach we took: trying to imagine the rise of a city out of a state of nature that I would have called imaginary if I had not seen something remarkably like it ten minutes earlier in the hallway. For the time being I found myself surprised to be appreciating the primal energy of adolescence, as I heard it identify more directly and vividly than adults ever would the variety of ways in which humans experience the need to gather in one place, which has always been, and still is, the reason for cities.

Having watched the students build the city from its raw and vital foundations, I ventured gingerly into the area of governance, asking them to describe what mechanisms they would provide to deal with the opportunities and challenges that this natural gathering in one place would inevitably present. This was clearly not entirely as much fun as imagining the gathering itself had been, but I was able to draw briefly on the reservoir of goodwill that had accumulated during the building phase. Having become rather fond of the city they had built, the students were willing to spend a little time providing it with police and fire protection, a sewer system, and enough streets to at least get them where *they* wanted to go. Something was troubling me, though, beyond the fear that the structure of government was about to smother the conversation.

As the students stocked their city with the necessary mix of basic services that occupied so much of my mayoral time, my mind slipped back to earlier conversations I had held with students here at Sentinel and in Missoula's other high schools. On several occasions, I had used invitations to speak to high school classes as an opportunity to ask teenagers how well the city worked for them. I suspected that I was about to do the same thing in this class, and I knew what I would hear, because it was what I always heard. "There's no place for us to get together in this town. Wherever we hang out, the police come and tell us to go someplace else. Where are we supposed to go?"

As I thought about introducing this conversation, with its inevitable conclusion, into my lesson on city government, I was suddenly struck by an obvious and embarrassing connection. I had asked these students to imagine how a city comes to exist because I knew what their answer would have to be: that cities exist because people both like and need to spend time together. Now, if I asked them for their one most vivid impression of their own city, I could be just as certain to hear once again about teenagers being dispersed by our police officers whenever and wherever they tried to come together. Their most salient experience of the physical city, I would be told, was that it lacked any appropriate place for them to hang out together.

I knew that teenagers always overstated this case, and that they would overstate it again today. There were many places in Missoula for them to go, and many places they enjoyed going. Still, the consistency of the refrain could hardly be ignored, and even if I recalled that my friends and I had said the same thing about another town a generation ago, I couldn't help feeling that this long-standing chorus of teenage complaints put my civics lesson somehow at risk. What good would it do to teach city government from the ground up, from the primal need of people to have a place to come together, if the central experience of teenagers was that their cities failed them precisely on this score?

I had learned during my years as mayor that I was by no means alone among city officials in feeling a growing concern about my city's relationship to its youngest residents. The persistent but relatively mild complaints of Missoula's teenagers might seem petty when compared to the conditions teenagers confront in large inner-city neighborhoods. But regardless of the setting, the way youth relate to their cities is becoming an urgent concern for large and small cities alike.

On the one hand, the steady rise in violence, so often perpetrated by teenagers or young adults, has contributed more than any other single factor to the flight of the affluent and the middle classes from central cities. The issues of youth gangs, teenage pregnancy, and adolescent drug and alcohol abuse are consistently mentioned as the most vexing problems confronting central city leaders. On the other end of the spectrum, those cities that have managed to maintain a reputation for livability are more and more inclined to measure that livability in terms of the city's "family friendliness" or by the standard of whether the city is a good place for raising children.

Like anyone faced with an urgent challenge, those who work on youth issues in the setting of a particular city tend to focus so closely on the task at hand that they often fail to take into account some larger context that might make their work more effectual and sustainable. In the case of youth issues, a slight shift in focus from the immediate problems often brings into relief as background the city itself. What emerges against that background is an appreciation for the mutual relationship between a city and its youngest citizens. Those who focus on the issues of "youth at risk" begin to understand that the city cannot attain its potential (and in some cases cannot even survive) unless it serves its children well. Conversely, they see that only a healthy, well-functioning, well-integrated city can hope to summon the resources to become what it should or would like to be for its children.

In one arena after another, this reciprocal relationship between the whole of the city and its parts becomes crucial to an effective public policy. Having spent so many decades thinking of cities in fragmented, bureaucratic terms, we do not readily ask how the emerging wholeness of the city, or the realization of the city's potential, might help in the pursuit of solutions to particular city problems. But this is where history becomes indispensable, enabling us to step back from the immediacy of what confronts us so that we can see our challenges in a more complete context. It was probably some hazy intuition of this that led me to begin my civics lesson at Sentinel High School by asking students to imagine the emergence of a city out of a state of nature. But even outside the classroom, the history of cities may have more to teach us than we would imagine about how cities and their children can most effectively relate to each other. In fact, one lesson that emerges clearly from this historical perspective is that the fundamental relationship between cities and youth has always centered on education, but education taken in a much broader context. A good city has always been one that teaches citizenship, in the deepest sense of the word, and such cities are not only teachers, but are themselves always learning how to be better cities.

As the Sentinel students talked and argued that morning about the historical emergence of cities, I could not resist reminding them of an incidental relationship between their school and an important chapter in the history of cities. Sentinel High's athletic teams are called the Spartans, so I asked what the students knew about the relationship of Sparta to its own youth. Not much, it turned out. As I began to describe some of the rigors of Spartan adolescence, their ignorance about their namesake turned into a modestly better informed ambivalence. The Spartan practice of taking teenagers seriously seemed attractive to them, but the corresponding discipline was clearly less appealing. Yet as I left the school that day, noticing anew the Spartan warrior on the gymnasium's facade, the question of how cities have created citizens seemed to have become more urgent than ever. I vaguely remembered something that Lycurgus, the founder of Sparta, had said on this subject, and that night I tracked it down in Plutarch's biography of Lycurgus. While he was known as the founder of the Spartan constitution, Lycurgus, unlike most famous lawgivers, had insisted that the most important laws not be written down. Helpful as this approach may have been in terms of reducing the number of lawyers, Lycurgus' reasons had more to do with maintaining what he saw as the fundamental relationship between the city and its children. Plutarch's compact formulation gives us a glimpse of how Lycurgus viewed the educational function of the good city:

> He thought that the most important principles, on which the city's welfare and health depended, if imprinted on the hearts of the citizens by training and habit, would remain more firmly fixed than by compulsion; and that this education of the young would turn each of them into a lawmaker himself.[1]

In other words, through the discipline by which it educated its youth, the city built into its children's very characters those elements that were crucial to the maintenance of the city, those elements that we generally think need to be expressed in laws and regulations. On this basis alone Lycurgus deserves his reputation as a great lawgiver, for he understood as we now all too rarely do how crucial is the relationship between the city and the creation of citizens.

The totalitarian nature of Spartan society leaves us justifiably uncomfortable with relying too heavily on Sparta as a model for the good city. But if we look at Athens and the classic struggle between Spartan totalitarianism and Athenian democracy, we find more similarities than differences in terms of the relationship between these two very different cities and their children.

There may never be a more powerfully concentrated description of the good city than that provided by Pericles in his funeral oration following an early battle of the Peloponnesian War. Pericles' job was to preside over the burial of the Athenian soldiers, but he did more than that. He began by describing the contours of Athenian civilization in unforgettable terms, and concluded that Athens had become "an education for all of Greece." Implicit in his argument lay the recognition that Athens could only have assumed that role by having been, for generations, an education to itself. The power of Pericles' speech lies in his way of weaving together a description of the good citizen, exemplified by the soldiers whose deaths he was commemorating, and the good city, for whom they had given their lives. His reference to education sums up his central theme: the good city has nurtured and maintained its excellence through the generations by continually addressing itself to the development of those traits of character that ensure that the child will become a constructive member of the city — will become, in other words, a good citizen.

The reason this still matters today, twenty-five hundred years after Pericles' speech, is that the decline of our cities is nowhere more urgently evident than in the fact that too many of our children no longer seem to have any sense of connection to the city, let alone any sense of responsibility for its well-being. And the fewer of its youth who display those character traits that hold the city together, the weaker the city becomes, both in general and in its capacity to instill those crucial traits of character. The weakening of the relationship between city and emerging citizen turns into a vicious cycle, creating more and more youth with no education in citizenship, and therefore more and more cities with a declining capacity to do anything about it.

Yet cities, by what sometimes seems to be little more than blind instinct, fight back against their own decline. Increasingly that battle for survival returns them to the ancient wisdom about the reciprocal relationship between the city and the education of citizens. If ancient Greek city-states seem too remote as models for the modern city in crisis, a wise contemporary observer of cities teaches us the same lesson. Jane Jacobs captures the timeless lesson with characteristic bluntness:

> In real life, only from the ordinary adults of the city sidewalks do children learn — if they learn it at all — the first fundamental of successful city life: People must take a modicum of public responsibility for each other even if they have no ties to each other. This is a lesson nobody learns by being told. It is learned from the experience of having *other people without ties of kinship or close friendship or formal responsibility* take a modicum of public responsibility for you.[2]

No one has done a better job than Jane Jacobs of showing how the life of city sidewalks in well-knit neighborhoods teaches these lessons, or how the life of asphalt jungles in quarters that were never designed to be well-knit teach opposite lessons. Her vibrant descriptions of neighborhoods that teach citizenship successfully should serve as the beacon toward which urban policies steer themselves. But where such neighborhoods do not now exist, they cannot be created by ordinance or executive order; they can only be brought about by incremental steps of healing, no one of which by itself can make the city whole. One such healing step, recognized in more and more cities, is the use of mentors as a key ingredient in repairing the city's relationship to its youth. Such mentoring is rarely described in Jane Jacobs's homely, down-to-earth terms. But the reason mentoring is becoming so popular a feature of the urban youth agenda is the same reason that captured the attention of Lycurgus, Pericles, and then Jane Jacobs: cities teach citizenship through adults mentoring children.

So it is that citizens of Eugene, Oregon, have developed a broad-based community initiative called Networking for Youth. Eugene's leaders brought together a wide range of youth service groups, all of which felt that youth problems were growing faster than their city's capacity to address them. As these people compared notes about what worked and what didn't, they discovered a surprisingly strong consensus that mentoring should be the keystone to any effort to improve conditions for the city's teenagers. Business groups, labor, schools, government, and minority groups all pledged to provide mentors to the program. Other cities as diverse as Utica, New York, and Rapid City, South Dakota, have also come to see mentoring as the keystone in making their cities better teachers of citizenship.

By itself, this widespread surge of interest in mentoring might be just one more technique in a long list of failed efforts to reverse the decline of urban youth culture. If it turns out otherwise, it will be because this rediscovery of mentoring has in fact not stood by itself, but has been part of the rediscovery of an even deeper wisdom. For, as Jacobs says, it is not only through the human activity on its sidewalks that the city teaches citizenship (or its reverse). The very sidewalks themselves teach such lessons, as the concerned citizens and leaders of Peoria, Illinois, have learned in confronting the alarming increase in gang activity in their small city.

The name of Peoria brings to mind the quintessence of Middle America, summed up in the well-worn question, "How will it play in Peoria?" So it is shocking, and yet sadly in keeping with its bellwether reputation, that Peoria has experienced a steadily worsening gang problem in recent years. Early in 1993 this pattern escalated sharply, with five gang-related murders occurring in the first six weeks of the year. This wave of violence focused community attention on the issue just as many gang or "nation" members began to see that this escalation was putting their own lives seriously at risk. Wallace "Gator" Bradley, a former nation member from Chicago, helped negotiate a truce between Peoria's two primary nations — the Vice Lords and the Gangster Disciples. One of the conditions of the truce was that the City of Peoria would work with the nations to address what gang leaders had identified as their chief concern: jobs for Peoria's young people.

A task force appointed by the mayor to pursue the city's commitment devised a program called Build Peoria, a collaborative effort to provide education, work force readiness skills, short-term jobs, and job training for at-risk teenagers. In spite of the crisis nature of their problem, the people who came together around this issue refused to be misled into narrow, quick-fix solutions. If Build Peoria makes a difference, it will be in no small part because of the connections its leaders have recognized within the web of social, economic, political, and physical features that together make a city. This complexity was clearly acknowledged in the way Peoria officials first described their problem. "Citizens have expressed concern about the high incidence of crime and violence," they noted,

> but most never witness a crime. What they see is a disinvestment in structures and properties. One broken window or uncared for lawn begets another. Soon the residents and businesses give up and cease to invest in the area. Crime targets these areas because no one fights it.

In other words, as the physical fabric of the city disintegrates, it teaches those who come in contact with it, and especially young people, a clear lesson: "Nobody cares about this block or about this neighborhood." Worse, it teaches that not caring, or even open destruction, is consistent with the life of the city.

What Peoria's leaders, including its gang leaders, have decided to try is a very different kind of teaching. Some of it is straightforward mentoring. By matching teenagers with union craftsmen, Peoria's leaders hope to teach a growing number of teenagers good work habits as well as specific job skills. Here again, as Jane Jacobs says, are lessons that "nobody learns by being told." The subtle satisfactions that can accompany good work can only be learned by experience. At the elbow of a good worker, a teenager can learn that those satisfactions are real, but that no shortcuts can be taken to reach them. Work is work, often hard work, and the satisfactions that may accompany it are not attainable apart from the discipline and perseverance and perspiration that comprise the ethic of work.

Build Peoria has added to its mentoring program another feature that makes it much more likely that these vital lessons will take. The program not only provides opportunities for supervised or mentored work, but also concentrates on tangible construction projects to repair the gang members' own neighborhoods, beginning with the repair of the very sidewalks upon which Jane Jacobs says citizenship is so often learned. As one of Build Peoria's designers put it, they want projects "that can be pointed to with pride while saying, 'I built that!'"

Peoria's leaders are rediscovering their own version of Lycurgus' and Pericles' wisdom. The pride of the young adult who might one day point out to his daughter or son a sidewalk or a front porch that he had built is precisely that kind of intentionally nurtured character trait that Lycurgus recognized as being something "on which the city's welfare and health depended," but which "if imprinted on the hearts of the citizens by training and habit, would remain more firmly fixed than by compulsion." What Lycurgus knew and what Peoria's leaders are grasping is that this teaching must come from the whole city, not from any one program, however well designed. Adults must teach it both in the indirect ways Jane Jacobs describes and through explicit mentoring programs such as Build Peoria. The physical city is also an indispensable teacher.

Just as Peoria learned how a broken window teaches that no one cares, it is now learning that a repaired sidewalk or front porch can teach very different kinds of lessons. These are lessons that the city and its citizens learn together as they engage in the work of healing each other. We are used to thinking of education as something the city supplies to its children in a specialized classroom setting. But the most successful cities seem to be those capable of seeing the community as a classroom, and indeed seeing the community as a kind of student, always engaged in broadening its own education. Nowhere does this education of the city take place more insistently than in the community that attempts to improve the conditions within which its young people live and grow toward adulthood. And it is not only cities struggling for their very survival that are learning these lessons. Communities noted for their livability, trying to maintain and enhance whatever makes them work, are coming to the same conclusions.

When the results of the 1980 Seattle census were analyzed, someone noticed that between 1970 and 1980 the population of Seattle had declined by 7 percent, but during the same decade the youth population had dropped by an astonishing 36 percent — more than double the average decline in other central cities in the country. As these statistics worked their way around the city, a handful of people began asking if there might be anything they could or should do about them.

The immediate result was a survey of sixty thousand Seattle schoolchildren, asking questions like what the respondents' favorite places in the city were, or what they would do to make Seattle a better place for kids if they were mayor. Based on the results of this survey, a committee, including representatives of the YMCA, the Junior League, and the city of Seattle, selected projects to receive financial support to make Seattle a "kids' place." Eight playgrounds were reopened as the result of the project, hours were increased at other recreation centers, and a weeklong celebration of and for Seattle's youth was launched, with waived or reduced admission to many of Seattle's major attractions and special events.

In the years following the establishment of Seattle's Kids-Place, word of this unusual initiative spread to distant quarters. I know now (although it escaped my attention at the time) that someone made a presentation about KidsPlace in Missoula in the mid-eighties. Nothing came of it here at the time, but other cities were ready for the message. In a small but important way, Seattle, like Pericles' Athens, had become an educational example for its sister cities, and in every case the lessons were of greatest value to those cities that were prepared to be educated themselves as they sought to become better teachers of their own children.

In 1986, a group of community activists in St. Louis, convinced that youth problems were growing steadily worse in spite of their best efforts, decided to give Seattle's approach a try. With the help of a grant from the Danforth Foundation, they set out to test the Seattle survey in St. Louis schools. Almost immediately they ran into problems. The field test of the Seattle survey met a less than enthusiastic response. Interviews with the youngsters included in the test sample revealed that many of them were more concerned with social issues than with the questions about places that had worked so well in Seattle. As they heard this response from more and more of the youth they were interviewing, the survey sponsors decided to redesign the questionnaire to allow it to capture the full range of young St. Louisians' concerns.

The committee now printed seventy thousand copies of the revised questionnaire. "We didn't know at the time that you don't have to survey everyone to get valid information," Blair Forlaw, the St. Louis KidsPlace director, explains with a self-deprecating chuckle. But the group's naiveté about the science of surveys proved to be a source of great strength. Even before they had begun analyzing the results, the sponsors found that they were learning more about St. Louis youth. They were surprised, almost flabbergasted, by the enthusiasm with which the youngsters responded to the survey. "The most important lesson of the survey didn't come in the data," Blair Forlaw told me. "Our most important lesson came from watching the enthusiasm of the kids about even being asked." The adults had expected a high percentage of flip or smart-aleck answers; in the end, they discarded an insignificant fifteen or twenty of the seventy thousand on that basis. "Just watching the students answer the survey showed us how interested they were," Forlaw says.

The survey sponsors were surprised again by the number of students who accepted the invitation to sign the survey if they wanted to be further involved in the project. Expecting at best a few hundred signatures, the sponsors found themselves overwhelmed by thousands of them. Now the question became what to do with all these kids who said they wanted to get more involved. Here again, the adults who had launched the project soon found themselves changing their expectations. "We began by thinking that our job was to figure out what the community could do for kids," Forlaw recalls. There is still a sense of wonder in her voice as she remembers how that perspective changed. "Slowly, as we sat at the same table with kids who said they wanted to get more involved, our consciousness changed, and we started to see that our job wasn't to do something for the kids but to help them figure out how they could contribute to the community."

Studying the survey results, the young volunteers readily identified a number of arenas within the city, ranging from drug and alcohol programs to the design of housing projects, that their peers had identified as needing improvement. Now the challenge would be to persuade the adults who reigned over those arenas to involve youth in a meaningful way. "Most adults have never had an experience of working with youth as equal partners," Forlaw explains. "At first you have to force them to do it because they can't see any value in it. But once they do it, they see immediately that teenagers are worth listening to."

Forlaw recalls with special delight urging a drug treatment program to bring in some teenagers to help figure out what might actually get kids not to use drugs. She finally persuaded the program managers that teenagers themselves might have something helpful to say on the subject, but the professionals were still dubious about actually inviting kids to one of their meetings. Finally, one of the directors turned to Forlaw and asked her, "Couldn't you just bring us a videotape of some teenagers?"

Time and again, the St. Louis experience presents this unexpected theme: what seems like a straightforward matter of designing and implementing a set of services for kids keeps turning into a challenge to adults to adjust their thinking, to learn new ways of doing things. The experience was repeated when Mayor Vincent Schoemehl, Jr., was persuaded to sponsor an all-day event to give youngsters a chance to get involved in the planning of a few key construction projects. KidsPlace organized the event, inviting what Blair Forlaw calls "the big cheeses, the movers and shakers" behind five different ventures to come to city hall and talk with kids about their plans.

At first the organizers thought they might have trouble getting teenagers to show up for this type of event, but that wasn't the problem. "It wasn't the kids who were intimidated," Forlaw recalls, "but the developers, who had never talked as professionals to kids before." Here again the event proved to be a learning experience as much for the adults as for the youngsters, as it became clear that these young citizens had perfectly valid contributions to make to the design of the projects. As a result, at least one of the ventures — the cultural and entertainment revitalization plan for downtown St. Louis known as the Grand Center — created an ongoing youth advisory group to make sure it works as well as possible for the youth of St. Louis.

But there are those who are certain to ask what real difference any of this can make. It may be all very well to give youngsters some kind of say in the design of Grand Center, but if at the same time even more children are born into poor, single-parent households, if there are more guns in the schools and even fewer middle-class families willing to live in the inner city, what difference will it have made?

In fact, by itself a program like St. Louis' KidsPlace will not succeed, nor will Build Peoria or Eugene's Networking for Youth or Waco's Lighted Schools program. But these programs are not happening by themselves; they do not exist in a vacuum. For one thing, these carefully devised youth programs in large and small cities across the country hint at a growing synergy, as cities become mentors to one another in their earnest desire to do better by their children. Even more important, in most of these cities there is a steadily growing awareness that youth programs must be seen and nurtured in a much broader context, one that finally becomes the context of the living city itself. The African aphorism that "it takes a village to raise a child" is quoted now in every quarter, revealing an awareness that if what is at stake is the wholeness and health of each child, it is only a whole and healthy community that can consistently produce such children. So, in Albany, Georgia, when a consortium of youth service providers decided that they were not getting the job done, they described precisely this relationship between the whole child and the whole community:

> We realize all aspects of our young people's lives — education, family needs, lack of personal goals, absence of job and leadership training, and a need for genuine encouragement and caring — must be addressed. And it takes more than either the city government or the schools alone can provide. Thus we came together to concentrate and unify our efforts, and empower and enable our community to address serious concerns.

Once again, an understanding of the living, organic nature of cities leads to the conclusion that no single part of the city can be healed in isolation, but, conversely, that good healing work on key sectors of the city can motivate the healing of other sectors closely related to it. Many cities wisely view their relations to their young people as a vital starting point in the overall healing of the city. Inevitably, this attention expands into other areas of the city's life.

It is remarkable, for example, how often a city's youth initiative turns its attention to the built environment — to the physical body of the city. Whether it is Peoria teaching job skills and good work habits by giving gang members a chance to repair the sidewalks and front porches of their neighborhoods or St. Louis developing a successful new cultural center for kids, cities are addressing the source of that uneasiness I felt in the Sentinel High classroom. Seldom in so many words, cities are remembering that the reason they exist at all is to enable people to gather in a humanly satisfying and sustaining way, and that children are more likely to become good citizens if their own city works that way for them.

But even when a city's youth program connects itself with a number of other aspects of the city's life, there is no guarantee that such a program will produce the results it seeks. Disappointing as the failure of a youth program can be, it can also be a learning experience, both for adults and for the young people they are preparing for citizenship. For it is not just our physical cities or our "youth service delivery systems" that need repair; the body politic itself is ailing, and one of its greatest maladies is its growing propensity to believe that there must be a quick, technical fix for any problem that arises. When elected officials fail to discover or to implement those simple solutions, we grow surly, or turn to political charlatans who tell us we have only to lift the hood and fix the engine.

This resort to a mythical quick fix undermines our political culture wherever it strikes. It is especially toxic when it arises in the context of cities addressing youth problems. Young people are already all too well trained in expecting everything in life to appear as effortlessly as a Big Mac, within seconds of its being ordered. The last thing we should be encouraging is a fast-food attitude toward politics. These approaches — mentoring, neighborhood repair projects, efforts by adults to work with teenagers on a more equal basis — are all hopeful and positive initiatives, but none of them, nor any combination of them, will "fix" the youth problems of a city. No single part of the city can be healed apart from an effort to make the city more whole. An important element of that effort should be teaching young people about the unavoidable complexities, uncertainties, and setbacks of politics.

"We can often be moved by young people's hopes and dreams," says Peg Michels, director of the Public Achievement Project at the Humphrey Center in Minneapolis, "but we don't call on them to deal with their issues in power terms — as serious participants." Michels's project trains mentors, or "coaches" — usually university students doing community service, who are looking for ways to become more politically effective. These coaches then work with teams of adolescents on problems the teenagers have identified. Among other things, they help them to "map" players and interests with a stake in the issue the teenagers have chosen to work on. "In the process, they acquire a more complex view of the people involved — beyond the stereotypes they may have started with," Michels explains.

In this mentored move from an oversimplified to a more realistically complex view of how things work, the teenagers often learn to see not only other people's but also their own roles in a different light. Michels tells about a church-based group of students who decided they wanted to address child abuse by putting on a play. They wrote the play and were getting ready to perform it when their adviser asked, "Are you going to show how kids could do anything about this problem?" "They hadn't thought about that at all," Michels said. "They were so used to moralizing about how bad the world is, and not ever going beyond that. Now they were motivated to rewrite the play to show themselves first in their old attitude of moralizing and complaining about their victimization and then moving beyond that to actually contributing to a solution."

From my experience as an elected official, having sat through more public hearings than I care to recall, I can think of nothing that would contribute more to the strengthening of the city than teaching people — whether youngsters or adults — to move beyond the moralizing of self-described victims to a willingness to find and implement solutions to the city's problems. What this requires, above all, is an expanding appreciation for the complexity and subtlety of those problems, and therefore an appreciation for the complexity and the subtlety of successful solutions. Without that appreciation, we will overlook many of the finely detailed ways in which cities are already healing themselves.

As the St. Louis KidsPlace organizers brought groups of youngsters together with citizen leaders to address the issues mentioned most frequently in their survey, they often arranged to hold the meetings around the big table in the city hall conference room. "We'd watch the kids get used to the room, finding out how the chairs squeaked, how far back they could tip," Blair Forlaw remembers. "There was something about the room, the huge table with the city seal in the middle of it, that created a sense of dignity and made the teenagers feel responsible when they sat around it." Forlaw recalls one meeting, several months after the survey, when an adult, new to this idea of meeting with teenagers, attempted to put the boy across the table from her at ease with a little small talk. "Have you ever served on a committee before?" she asked him. "Oh, yes," he assured her, "I've sat at this table many times."

This is the type of education upon which good cities have always depended. Plutarch describes how another table, Sparta's common dining table, played a crucial role in preparing Spartan citizens:

> Boys were taken to the public tables as schools of good manners and temperance. There they listened to political debates and so were instructed in statecraft. There they learned to talk easily, to joke without vulgarity, and to take jokes without loss of temper.[3]

It may seem frivolous, in the face of gang murders in cities as small as Peoria, to speak of how the chairs squeak around a St. Louis conference table, let alone how Spartan youth twenty-five centuries ago had learned "to take jokes without loss of temper." Our urban crises call for solutions that are immediate, direct, effective, and reliable; we don't have time to worry about table manners. But, in fact, nothing is more important than understanding how, in a thousand subtle ways, the good city teaches precisely such fundamental lessons of citizenship.

One day, near the end of a Farmers' Market season, having finished my shopping but not yet being willing to relinquish the pleasures of the bright fall morning, I sat near the edge of the market, trying to understand how the quiet music of a single violin seemed to create a space within which people could move more easily and gracefully across the plaza. Again, Abe was with me, and it was he who drew my attention to the musician herself. Intent on the effect of her music, I had failed to notice that the performer was Vanessa, a classmate of Abe's at Sussex School. Now that I knew who was playing, my own relationship to the music began to change, and before long I got up and crossed to the bandstand to show in some small way my support and encouragement.

I sat for some time on the steps of the small bandstand, turning once to congratulate Vanessa on a difficult piece, and making her smile by recognizing (or correctly guessing) that it was Bach she had been playing. From where I sat I could see Vanessa's mother just across the way, deep in conversation with a woman I didn't know, not seeming to pay any direct attention to her daughter's performance, but obviously there, as I was, in support of this brave venture into public by a rather bashful teenager. As I sat, I noticed a number of other parents from Sussex School seeming drawn to the area of the bandstand, none making a fuss over Vanessa, probably moved more by wanting to hear her music than anything else, but unmistakably, like her mother and me, there to support her.

Now Abe, who had remained seated across the market-place when I moved to the bandstand, began to make his way over. At first I thought he was coming to join me, but then I saw that he had noticed his (and Vanessa's) social studies teacher, with her new baby in a stroller, among the Sussex parents and students who were congregating in front of the bandstand. As I watched Abe preparing to pay his respects to his teacher and her new baby, I was reminded of how often I saw scenes like this at the market, and it occurred to me that this had become, in fact, a kind of sacrament.

Within days of its birth, any summer child born to a regular market-going family would be brought out, introduced to the world, exclaimed over. But there was more to it than that, as I realized now, watching Abe partaking of this ceremony. Here was the secular equivalent of baptism, at least in that sacramental aspect of asking and receiving both the community's blessing upon the child and its commitment to take responsibility for the preparation of the child to become in due course a full member of the community. No one ever said as much, of course, but watching Abe reach out his finger to see if the baby could grasp it, I had no doubt that the gathering force of the market had, over its twenty years, evolved a ritual of initiation that at its best marked the beginning of citizenship.

THREE

The Character of the City

... for years
They wandered as their destiny drove them on
From one sea to the next: so hard and huge
A task it was to found the Roman people.

— VIRGIL, *Aeneid*

F LORA STREET STRETCHES for three or four blocks between the Dallas Museum of Art and the spectacular I. M.
Pei edifice of Symphony Hall. Anchored at either end by these
two landmarks, the "arts district," as envisioned in Dallas's
early 1980's urban renewal plan, was to be filled in by shops,
galleries, restaurants, and artists' housing. Urban renewal was
well under way in the early eighties, but it was renewal of a
kind that would eventually delay if not stymie altogether the
dreams for the arts district. Immediately across Flora Street
from the proposed district rose a number of shiny office towers, drawing the center of commercial activity outward from its
old locus along Main Street, and inevitably in the process
driving land prices so high that none of the plans for artists'
housing or anything else have yet been realized. The lots between the museum and the symphony that were to be filled
with art and related activities stand filled instead with cars, the
land held by speculators waiting for the next wave of high-rise
commercial construction to redeem their investments.

It may be a long wait. Across Flora Street from these parking lots, the Trammell Crow Center casts not only its literal
shadow but also the chilling influence of its own descent into
bankruptcy, as the golden glow of Ronald Reagan's Morning
in America, darkening to the savings and loan crisis, revealed
the hollowness of so much of the speculative boom of the
eighties. Those who gambled on the boom spreading across
Flora Street have begun to wonder when, if at all, their investments will pay off. Perhaps nothing more poignantly captures
their plight than the choice of sculpture placed at the Flora
Street entrance to the Trammell Crow Center. In the building's
lobby, a number of Rodin sculptures testify to the seemingly
limitless Texas wealth that built this and its companion towers,
but out at the Flora Street entrance, Bourdelle's "Penelope"
broods and waits, gazing across the vacant lots, weaving some
of their dust into cobwebs between her folded arms. Probably
only a handful of those who pass into the Trammell Crow
Center on any given day notice who this figure is, or remember
the story of Penelope, waiting for years for Odysseus' return
from the Battle of Troy, holding at bay by determination and
craft the troop of suitors who refuse to leave her courtyard
until she gives up Odysseus for dead and agrees to marry one
of them. For those who do remember anything of the story, this
Lone Star Penelope may well seem to dream the dreams of the
unrealized arts district, wondering silently when the vision
might come to life, while the impatient suitors camped in her
courtyard ask themselves daily how long they can bear the
carrying charges on their parking lots.

    This, at least, was the image that came to mind as I sat one
May morning on the steps at Penelope's feet, trying to gain
some understanding of what had gone wrong with the plans
for the Dallas arts district. No doubt the company I was keeping that morning had channeled my thoughts in such direc-

tions. I had come to Dallas as a guest of the Dallas Institute of Humanities and Culture to participate in its annual What Makes a City conference, scheduled at city hall the next day. This year's conference theme was "the Sacred Center," and our walk through downtown Dallas was meant to train our minds on the center of this city which the Institute had made the focus of its work. Walking and talking had become one of the Institute's hallmarks; in fact, the psychologist James Hillman, one of the Institute's founders, once presented a paper to the Institute entitled "Talking as Walking," in which he argued that the word "conversation" itself "means turning around with, going back, like reversing, and it comes supposedly from walking back and forth with someone or something, turning and going over the same ground from the reverse direction. A conversation," Hillman concluded, "turns things around."[1]

During my brief stay in Dallas, I would learn how intensely involved the Institute of Humanities and Culture had become in turning things around in Dallas, often by "going over the same ground in the reverse direction." I myself would experience a certain amount of "turning around" as I walked and talked with the members of the Institute and their other guests. My own image of Dallas, for example, contained no "sacred center," but before I left the city, this along with many of my other preconceptions about the city would be left behind. Already here at Penelope's feet, my hosts were teaching me to see a far different city than the Dallas of my mind.

If being hosted by an organization devoted to humanities and culture had put me in a frame of mind to pay more attention than I might otherwise have done to such objects as Bourdelle's sculpture, I soon realized that the sculpture itself was also influencing how I saw the city. That I now found myself gazing at parking lots as if through the eyes of the patient Penelope was the direct result of there being a likeness of Penelope here at all. If such public sculpture is part of what we mean by a city's "culture," then that culture was already influencing my experience of the city, and must therefore be presumed to have influenced others' experience of it as well.

Still, how realistic is it to think that the three-thousand-year-old story of Penelope and Odysseus could have any actual relevance to the fact, announced just that morning, that the Trammell Crow Center (and with it, presumably, Penelope herself) had been placed in Chapter 11 bankruptcy? The question of culture that Dallas faced was whether this latest in a long series of commercial failures would doom still further the prospects of the arts district. What Penelope might think about it seemed more than a little beside the point.

Yet, whether it was my hosts' concentration on issues of culture or Bourdelle's skill in crafting such a credibly wistful Penelope, I found myself thinking of how another raw and muscular city, at a period of intense strain and change, had itself reached back to the Battle of Troy and its aftermath to fashion a clearer understanding of what that city's struggles might mean and how it might best address those issues. Homer had been many, many centuries dead when Virgil turned to the Homeric myths for material with which to retell Rome's story, to retell the story in a way that would make some sense of the change from republic to empire, which was challenging everything ordinary Romans thought they knew about their city. The story Virgil was to tell in the *Aeneid* would prove powerful enough to help Rome not only to weather the tumultuous years of Nero and Caligula, but also to incorporate the world-changing force of Christianity that was germinating in the Roman colony of Palestine as Virgil composed his poem. In fact, the *Aeneid* would prove so telling a tale of the human condition that its relevance would extend far beyond Rome: Dante would make Virgil a character in his *Inferno,* as he sought to help fourteenth-century Florence come to terms with its own historic struggles and opportunities. What gave Virgil's work such power was, in part, the fact that he was willing to reach beyond the horizons of his own city's history and draw upon the myths of another age as he reframed Rome's story, leaving its founder, Aeneas, to wander the world in search of a new homeland after the Greeks, guided by the crafty Odysseus, had finally sacked Troy. So the *Aeneid* became a Roman parallel to the *Odyssey,* as Virgil describes Aeneas' adventures on his way to what would become Rome.

But in addition to the narrative power that Virgil harnessed by recourse to the ancient myth of Troy, he unleashed an even greater power by using that myth to confront much of what Rome would rather not have admitted about itself. Having acknowledged Rome's roots in Greek civilization by drawing on the Homeric tradition, Virgil immediately creates (or admits) an internal struggle in the Roman soul by making the founder of Rome not a Greek but an enemy of the Greeks — Aeneas, descendant of the kings of Troy. Then, as if to insist on this need for Rome to come to terms with its enemies and with the ways it internalized its enmities, Virgil has Aeneas stop in Carthage, the city that was to Rome what Troy had been to Greece. Here Aeneas falls in love with Dido, the Carthaginian queen, so that only through an act of will contrary to the promptings of his heart could he leave Carthage and carry out the founding of Rome. Bitter as its struggle with Carthage may have been, Virgil implies, Rome cannot move on to the next stage of its own history until it comes to grips with the complexity of that relationship, which may have always had more than a trace of fascinated attraction mixed into its hatred.

Whenever a city undergoes great change, as Rome was certainly doing in Virgil's time and as Dallas is now doing, some accounting for the past, including the dark side of the

city's history — even the coming to terms with one's enemies
— is indispensable. As our walking tour of Dallas proceeded, I
would learn of the city's remarkable efforts to come to terms
with its own past, its own hatreds and bloodstains. I would
learn, too, that it was not the myth of Penelope and Odysseus,
but another Greek myth, the myth of Pegasus, that Dallas was
using to help it understand and move beyond its struggles.

I would continue to carry in the back of my mind the image
of Penelope waiting for the arts district to materialize while
speculators still camped on her doorstep. This image was
clouded, though, by the fact that no one actually hovers on
Penelope's doorstep, nor anywhere else in the immediate vicinity. The day I walked this neighborhood with a dozen or so
other guests of the Dallas Institute of Humanities and Culture,
I found myself gradually engulfed by a sense of something
strange, almost eerie. Here were these huge office towers
which had, we were told, drawn all the life out of Main Street,
but down here on Flora Street and the other avenues connecting these giants, there was simply no street life at all. Our little
group would walk for blocks at a time without encountering
more than three or four other people — and this on a working
weekday. I had been especially excited about this trip to Dallas
from the moment I heard that both Jane Jacobs and Christopher Alexander were to be among the Dallas Institute's guests,
and that we were all going to spend a day walking the downtown streets together. I spent weeks imagining myself listening
to these sage observers of cities talk about how Dallas's downtown street life and streetscape related to and enlivened each
other. But now, since it turned out that there was no street life,
there was little either of them could say on that subject beyond
wondering what had happened to all the people.

It was only after lunch at the Dallas Aquarium that we
found the answer. Our guides had decided that we would now

make our way toward Main Street, not at street level, but under the streets. We descended, then, into what proved to be a network of underground pedestrian passageways connecting several of the office towers and parking garages of the district. Here, in the shops, restaurants, and passages of this gargantuan underground mall, we found at last the tens of thousands of people whose presence we had so acutely missed on the streets above. "It's like a movie about life after a nuclear war," Robert Sardello, one of the Institute's founders, murmured. I had already fixed on a slightly different image, evoked by having read C. S. Lewis's *Chronicles of Narnia* over and over again to my children: here, in the flesh, was the underground city so chillingly described in *The Silver Chair*.

We emerged at last to the havoc and hubbub of Main Street, torn up from one end to the other for a major face-lifting as part of a concerted effort to revitalize the old heart of the city. Here we were joined by Kent Collins, the director of the Main Street Project, who told us that Dallas was the first city of its size in the country to tap into the National Trust for Historic Preservation's Main Street Program, which had been so effective a component of downtown revitalization efforts in dozens of smaller cities. Could anything of that kind happen in a city like Dallas, where Texas-sized speculation next door had gutted the old heart of the city? Neither Collins nor anyone else involved in the project seemed to be suffering any illusions about the magnitude of the challenge. Collins had clearly been driven rather frantic by the ceaseless need to reassure the hundreds of shop owners who still operated along Main Street that the maddening disruption to their businesses caused by all this sidewalk, sewer, and street construction would pay off for them in the long run, if they could just hold on until it was completed.

Back at the Dallas Institute that night, we would be served a fine dinner catered by one of the Main Street restaurants. This was one of what I learned were numerous examples of the supporters of the Main Street project doing whatever little they could to help these entrepreneurs weather the effort to bring more life and with it more business back to their neighborhood. But the Dallas Institute had other plans for assisting Main Street's resurrection, and we were about to see what they were.

The object of our pilgrimage up Main Street, with its countless detours around sewer trenches and mud puddles, was the Magnolia Building. It is one of many that now stands empty above its ground floors, all its activity drained into the more commodious towers that, despite their inability to pay for themselves, have drawn Dallas's commercial center away from Main Street. The city's commercial center of gravity had shifted only a matter of a few blocks, but the effect here, on Main Street, was unmistakable and dramatic.

Earlier, in the shadow of one of the new glass towers on Flora Street, I had imagined Penelope and her story into the current saga of downtown Dallas, but here at the Magnolia, another Greek myth has come to occupy a central role in the efforts to reclaim the center of Dallas from the devastation wrought by the boom of the eighties and its painful aftermath. The statue of Pegasus, the winged steed forever ascending from the roof of the Magnolia Building, had captured the attention and imagination of generations of Dallas residents and visitors. Gail Thomas, now the director of the Dallas Institute of Humanities and Culture and our chief guide on this downtown tour, recalled how as a girl growing up in rural Texas she used to hang over the front seat of her parents' car as it approached Dallas on the family's rare visits to the city, straining to be the first to catch a glimpse of Pegasus' red glow atop the Dallas skyline.

Before the glass-encased skyscrapers began overwhelming it in the seventies, the Dallas skyline had long been dominated by the Magnolia. When it was built in the early twenties, the Magnolia was the tallest building south of St. Louis, and proud of it. In the early thirties, Magnolia Oil, which would eventually become Mobil Oil, added to the building's height and visibility by affixing to the roof its corporate symbol, the multi-ton, neon-outlined steel Pegasus. By the time Gail Thomas began to identify the horse with the city, the city itself had already done the same. Magnolia Oil probably did not mind that its corporate symbol had become the city's own hallmark, but whether it minded or not was by now beside the point, since Pegasus and Dallas had become part of each other.

Gail Thomas, like many another rural Texas child, eventually moved into the city. As her career there matured, the city changed, and Pegasus came to be dwarfed by the steel and glass giants surrounding it. Thomas, already a student of the city, noticed the regret so often expressed in letters to the editor or streetside conversations about the eclipse of the flying red horse. But for her, as for most people, this was soon accepted as the price of change, and for a time Pegasus sank below her mental horizon as it had below Dallas's changing skyline.

By the mid-seventies, Gail Thomas had become the director of the Center for Civic Leadership at the University of Dallas. There, and later as the director of the Dallas Institute, she organized seminars and workshops to explore questions of what actually makes a city work for the people who inhabit it. The sessions she organized were so well presented, and the outside speakers she invited so stimulating, that Thomas and the Institute earned a solid and credible reputation among many of Dallas's more farsighted and thoughtful civic leaders. But the Institute was always pushing people to look beneath the surface of the city, to something of deeper significance.

"We endured a lot of ridicule, and became accustomed to seeing people roll their eyes when we would start talking about 'the soul of the city,'" Thomas recalls. Among the Institute's founders and fellows, psychologists James Hillman and Robert Sardello sought to bring their insights to bear on the life of the city. Above all, they continually urged the citizens who attended their "What Makes a City" discussions to think about the role of myth in the city's struggle with its past and with the challenges of its future.

To the outside world, Dallas was, during the Institute's early years, a myth in its own right. The television series that bore the city's name spoke to a deepening strain of cynicism as the baby-boom generation moved into that phase of its journey that would earn it, at least temporarily, the title "the Me Generation." J. R. Ewing's unrelenting self-centeredness presented the sharpest possible contrast to the idealism so prevalent in the early sixties. In fact, that very contrast led many observers to speculate that the series' setting had been perfectly chosen, since it was in Dallas that the idealism of "a new generation of Americans" had been so brutally cut down. Whatever role the Kennedy assassination may have played in the larger American psychodrama, its impact on Dallas was far more concentrated and far more subject to denial and repression.

But it was just such repression that Hillman, Sardello, and the other members of the Dallas Institute were determined to avoid. Hillman once identified the role of the Institute as "keeping a conversation going and not letting things remain unsaid, unspoken, repressed."[2] The Institute was founded on the premise that "humanities and culture" were not just words, or academic constructs, but that if they meant anything at all, their meaning had to be sought in and brought to bear on the real life of the real city. Its founders had staked their livelihoods on that proposition, leaving behind secure aca-

demic positions and devoting themselves instead to the very
real life of the city they called home.

As they moved their work from the campus into the heart
of the city, and began engaging Dallas civic leaders and outside
observers of cities in discussions about "what makes a city,"
the image of Pegasus began once again to command Gail Thomas's attention, as it had when she rode with her family into
the city years before the Book Depository and the grassy knoll
had replaced Pegasus and the Magnolia as Dallas's leading
landmarks. Thomas now began to ask herself whether the
story of Pegasus might shed any light on the trauma Dallas had
suffered, and on the often cynical way the city had chosen to
deal with that trauma.

Thomas would eventually write a monograph about Pegasus and Dallas, reminding people that behind the image
rising from the roof of the Magnolia building lay a story that
had borne meaning to generations of people in other cities long
ago. The ancient Greeks had told and retold the story of Pegasus springing to life from the head of the Medusa, whose
deadly gaze had for so long turned all who came under it to
stone. Finally the hero, Perseus, is guided to slay the Medusa
by looking at her, not directly, but in the reflection of his shield.
Through an act that Thomas calls "of enormous boldness, risk
and reflection," Perseus succeeds in slaying the Medusa, and
out springs Pegasus. Soaring and swooping with energy and
new life, Pegasus at last alights, and where his hoof first strikes
the ground, a well springs up. Around it the nine Muses
gather, bringing into the world art, music, poetry, and all the
refinements of civilization.

Dallas learned the hard way that simply by designating an
arts district, it could not make the muses appear. What Thomas
argues is that if the story of Pegasus is in any way Dallas's own

story, then before the muses could appear, "We have to realize what the Medusa is; we have to know the thing that turns us to stone, that freezes us with fear, so that we can't act." Thomas was convinced that the myth of Pegasus was in fact Dallas's story, because, as she puts it, "We continue to rise out of impossible odds."

Thomas has retold the story of Dallas in these terms, in a way that refuses to deny the fearful, turning-to-stone events that have so often marked the city's history. She recalls that John Neely Bryan had arrived at the Three Forks of the Trinity River in 1841, just two weeks after all the native Cherokee Indians had been massacred at the site Bryan would plat as the beginning of Dallas. Thomas compares this "first founding" of Dallas with what she calls its "second founding," following a different kind of massacre. "After the Kennedy assassination," Thomas recalls, "after the city suffered that horror and the further horror of being blamed for it all over the world, Mayor Erik Jonsson led the rebuilding — really the refounding — of Dallas, because of his determination to overcome the blight on Dallas's name." Under Jonsson's leadership, a new city hall was built, a new public library, and all the skyscrapers which would eventually dwarf the Magnolia Building and the statue of Pegasus.

Powerful as those boom years were in the history of Dallas, they created their own Medusa-like effect, hardening the city, driving its street life away from the old center, driving it in fact underground, beneath and up into gigantic buildings that could not, in the end, sustain themselves, but which fell one by one into bankruptcy and foreign ownership, even as Dallas's three major locally owned banks were taken over by outside interests. This was the situation into which the story of Pegasus was reintroduced into Dallas's own unfolding story.

As the effect of the new office towers on the old life of the city settled into a clearly worsening pattern of downtown decay, a new set of civic and elected leaders began to emerge, in what Gail Thomas calls the "collapse of the patriarchy," the white male–dominated oligarchy that had governed Dallas for generations. As a new set of leaders, including Dallas's first woman mayor, began to assess the city's situation, they decided that business as usual was no longer serving the city well, and that some new approaches would have to be tried. Massive urban renewal efforts of the kind that had produced the Trammell Crow Center or Symphony Hall could not be repeated, even if anyone was inclined to do so, because the money was simply not there to do it. Instead, civic and elected leaders began to encourage some of those modest but well-placed projects, which Christopher Alexander describes as "increments of construction . . . made in such a way as to heal the city."

As so often happens, these small acts of healing the physical body of the city became acts of civic healing as well, and here, as in so many cities, the impetus came from citizen leaders. One example is Fair Park, site of both the Texas State Fair and the Margo Jones Theater. Mary Ellen Degnan, president of the Friends of Fair Park, led the effort to renovate and restore the old theater, now known as the Magnolia Lounge. Observing this and other healing acts of construction, the Dallas Institute decided in effect to up the ante.

With the help of grants from the Dallas Foundation and the National Endowment for the Arts, in 1986 the Institute launched a five-year effort to envision how the healing of Dallas might expand into the city at large. The project was named Dallas Visions, and to direct it, the Institute hired Degnan. She brought to the effort lessons learned and enthusiasm gained in the restoration of Fair Park and the Magnolia Lounge. To Gail Thomas, whose work on Pegasus she had read, Degnan brought a tiny replica of the sculpture capping the old theater: another statue of Pegasus.

Dallas Visions, involving hundreds of citizens and dozens of designers and planners, eventually recommended a major effort to revitalize the old commercial center of Dallas along Main Street and its adjoining avenues. In time, city government was persuaded of the wisdom of this suggestion, and prepared a formal request for engineers, architects, and developers to propose methods of revitalizing the center of Dallas. Among the sixty responses to the request came one from Louis Salcedo, an engineer who had caught some of the civic spirit of Dallas Visions from working on one of its earlier projects. Intrigued by his experience with Jubilee Park, Salcedo decided to ask the Dallas Institute itself to help with the design of the Main Street project, and to choose the architects for it. Together, they came to the conclusion that the Magnolia Building, at the corner of Main and Akard, should be the focus of the revitalization project, and that Pegasus, who still rose as he had for sixty years from the Magnolia's roof, should be invited, at least figuratively, to come down to earth.

At the foot of the Magnolia lay a now vacant lot, into which Pegasus' shadow sometimes fell, and here Salcedo and his team began to imagine what would eventually become Pegasus Plaza. With the help of architect Larry Good and landscape architect Luis Santana, the Institute prepared a proposal for a plaza that was centered around a fountain tapping a natural spring underlying the lot, a spring that had been capped since the early sixties. The fountain was designed to suggest the creative energy released when Pegasus' hoof strikes the ground; from the fountain, a stream would be channeled in the shape of the constellation named for Pegasus, flowing past ancient stones quarried from Texas earth, each representing one of the nine Muses.

This was the heart of the proposal that Salcedo brought before a public works panel charged with selecting the best approach to revitalizing the heart of downtown Dallas. Into this room full of hard-bitten realists, Gail Thomas carried her article about Pegasus, and to this panel she argued that Dallas, after all it had been through, "needed more than fancy brick-work and street trees; we need to bring the real spirit of Dallas back to life." Braced for the rolling of eyes to which the Institute had become accustomed when it used such language, Thomas was delighted when, as she tells it, "One old boy leaned forward and asked, 'And what are the names of the nine Muses?'" "I knew he was hooked," Thomas recalls, "and I felt the hair stand up on the back of my neck." What gripped Thomas's attention at that moment was not that this crusty old Texan had suddenly stepped out of character, but that he had been given and had responded to a meaningful way of under-standing his city's, and perhaps his own, story. "As people who have known Dallas for a long time hear the story of Pegasus as the story of Dallas, they're almost always taken by it," Thomas says. Looking around the table at the panel that would decide on the shape of Main Street's revitalization, Thomas felt "as if they had the image of Pegasus reflected in their eyes." Salcedo and the Institute won the contract, and in the fall of 1994, Pegasus Plaza was officially dedicated, its fountain enlivening the Dallas streetscape with the long-buried water of its hidden spring.

Will Pegasus Plaza make a difference in what happens to downtown Dallas? Will the $2 million the city invested there prove worthwhile? It may never be possible to answer these questions with scientific certainty; art, after all, is not science, but the healing and strengthening of cities is much more of an art than a science. Rolling eyes and raised eyebrows will always greet those who urge a city to risk something like Pegasus Plaza, and the most hard-bitten skeptics will always be those who need to believe that facts, data, and money alone can move a city forward. But the wholeness of a city rests in no small part on the recognition that, like a human being, a city cannot live on bread alone, any more than it can live without attention to the basic needs of life.

David Dillon, the architecture critic for the *Dallas Morning News*, had argued that "the problems of downtown Dallas are not going to be solved by a single plaza," and that the city must pursue "practical solutions, such as business development and a housing policy."[3] But successful cities are those that learn to move beyond this false dichotomy between that which is merely cultural and that which is merely practical. Of course a single plaza cannot "fix" Dallas, but who can measure the incremental effect such a place might have on those very issues of housing and economic development which critics like Dillon would make the center of the city's efforts?

In fact, as Dallas joins a lengthening list of cities recognizing that people informing and educating one another may be to the new economy what physical production has been to the old, the business, or "busyness," of a good downtown begins to take on quite a new look. Midway through the construction of Pegasus Plaza, a consortium of universities and colleges from the greater Dallas region announced the beginning of construction of the Downtown Education Center at the old Joske Building, three blocks up Main Street from the plaza. Designed to serve those among the 117,000 downtown workers and 312,000 residents of central Dallas who might want to further their education without leaving their living or working neighborhood, the Downtown Education Center is almost certain to increase the number of people who both live and work near the center of town. Graham Greene, the designer of the project, is already making plans to add to the education center both residential and retail space at the Main Street site.

The idea of encouraging people to live downtown is catching the attention of several developers, including those planning the renovation of the old Kirby Building office tower at Main and Akard, just across the street from Pegasus Plaza. Both the Kirby and the Joske renovations have included downtown residential space in their plans because the downtown, by adding congenial gathering places like Pegasus Plaza, is promising to become a more attractive place to live. And if the Kirby does indeed become a 194-unit residential building, its inhabitants will inevitably add to the life and liveliness Gail Thomas and others envision for Pegasus Plaza. "I hope we'll see people coming out of their offices, condominiums, and apartments, walking and sitting at the plaza, buying from street vendors, listening to live music," Thomas told me. The plaza's fountain has been designed so that it can be turned off and transformed into a stage for music, theater, or even oratory. In fact, the Dallas Institute intends to encourage the use of the stage for a storytelling series, since the plaza itself grew out of an expanding appreciation for how the story of Pegasus and the story of Dallas fed into each other. If stories really do matter in a city, then there should be some place in the city where storytelling is encouraged.

But Gail Thomas is a wise enough observer of cities, and above all of her own city, to know that a city's story unfolds out of itself, not according to anyone's plan, and that the same must be true of any vital part of a city, as Pegasus Plaza is meant to be. So what happens in the plaza cannot be planned; at best it can provide a stage upon which the city might continue to unfold its story. Nothing would please Gail Thomas more than that, and nothing would signal more surely the success of the plaza.

Of all the forms of art that a good city might promote, perhaps none is of such symbolic importance as the theater — the city providing itself a stage upon which its own story is allowed to unfold. Virgil's story of the founding of Rome illustrates this central role of theater. Virgil has Aeneas arrive in Carthage just as the city is being founded. The busyness of the city is remarkable — bee-like, as Virgil describes it — but at the heart of that busyness is the city's creation of its own stage:

Laws were being enacted,
Magistrates and a sacred senate chosen.
Here men were dredging harbors, there they laid
The deep foundation of a theatre,
And quarried massive pillars to enhance
The future stage — as bees in early summer
In sunlight in the flowering fields
Hum at their work, and bring along the young
Full-grown to beehood.[4]

Laws and commerce are now, as they were in Virgil's time, universally recognized as integral to the existence of a city; however, no less integral to the foundation of a good city is theater — the stage around which the city gathers to view its most challenging dimensions in a different light. This is why Athens at the peak of its civilization is simply unimaginable without Sophocles or Euripides. "For it was in the theater," Lewis Mumford argues, "that the Greek citizen saw himself and obeyed the Delphic maxim: Know Thyself."[5] The stage is indispensable to the city because it represents the city in microcosm. So even today, cities that engage in rediscovering their human potential turn with remarkable regularity to the building or reclaiming of theaters. Whether it is the Margo Jones Theater in Dallas, the Kentucky Theater in Lexington, the Tivoli in Chattanooga, the Bagley Wright Theater at Seattle Center, or the Wilma Theater in Missoula, the care that cities and their citizens focus on their theaters tells us all we need to know about the indispensable role of culture as a medium between the good city and the good life.

Almost without exception, theaters or theater districts are found at the city's center, which means among other things that the theater's design becomes a matter of elemental concern within the framework of city design. Here the visual and the performing arts invariably intersect, as architecture and drama challenge and invigorate each other. Here too the city's history often becomes an issue, as the theater situates itself within its historically determined surroundings. In the realms of theater, architecture, and history, Mumford traces the path we have already noted in literature, from Homer's Greece through Virgil's Rome to Dante's Florence:

> Even today, on the hillside of Fiesole near Florence, the semi-circle of stone benches looking over the valley that spreads below and the mountains that rise beyond, recaptures the all but universal form of the Greek theater, and exhales a faint breath of the original culture that produced it. The beauty of ordered space within an ordered cosmos.[6]

And "even today," as any city follows Virgil's Carthage in laying "the deep foundation of a theater," it invariably discovers that "culture" is not finally something remote, ancient, and inaccessible, but something that arises from, even as it sinks its foundations into, the very life of the city itself. Always, in the living city, the web of culture comes down to earth in countless ways, situating people in a dynamic balance between their innermost aspirations and struggles and the world they find themselves inhabiting. Nowhere does this situating work draw more directly from the city's own roots than in the theater — even in a city as small and remote as Missoula.

My own experience of theater in Missoula has centered mainly around two stages: the Missoula Children's Theater and the Wilma. Throughout my tenure as mayor of Missoula, I waited for the day the city government would find a way to invest in the restoration of the old Wilma Theater. Before that day arrived, however, the Wilma would become a major factor in my ongoing political education, teaching me patience as nothing else had ever done, but also teaching me in totally unsuspected ways the meaning of theaters and of theater in the life of a city.

In the heart of downtown Missoula, right next to the riverfront, the Wilma Building had, since its construction in the 1920s, always served a variety of functions. Its seven-story residential tower, divided into some of the funkiest apartments in the city, had been home to a slowly shifting stream of residents whose often unusual identities blended with the character of the old building itself. It was rumored that David Lynch, who included some offhand references to Missoula in the script for *Twin Peaks*, had once lived in one of these apartments. Whether the story was true or not, it worked better than anything else we could think of to explain what was the subtly offbeat Missoula influence on that prime-time soap opera. Living in one of those apartments, or riding to and from it in what must surely be the last elevator in the Northern Rockies still run by a personal attendant, seemed as good a place as any to begin accounting for Lynch's uniquely oblique view of everyday life. But if the upper reaches of the Wilma inspired theatricality, its nether regions lived, breathed, and defined theater, Missoula-style.

At street level, the main theater served on most nights as a second-run movie house, gently rebuking the sterile shoeboxes of the first-run sixplexes with its chandeliers, fabric-covered walls, and tiered balconies. Here Missoulians gathered for full-house performances by the Missoula Symphony Orchestra; here thousands of children watched live performances of the Nutcracker every December, and here the Missoula Children's Theater staged major performances by both its children and adult casts to audiences too large for its smaller home theater on Front Street. The Wilma, in short, had become Missoula's premier performing arts center, and as market pressures and the cost of fire code compliance almost forced Missoula to destroy the Wilma by triplexing it, patrons of the performing arts began mounting countervailing pressure on city hall to rescue the theater.

More than amenable to such pressure, I steadily supported our downtown redevelopment agency in its policy of setting aside funds for the eventual restoration of the theater. We were prepared to invest up to a million dollars in the task, expecting that in the process the city would become the owner of the theater, thereby assuring its continued use as a community performing arts center. But here my lessons in patience began, as I entered into a series of discussions with Ed Sharp, principal owner of the Wilma Building. While Mr. Sharp's domain ranged throughout the building, including the main theater at street level, he was best known to the Missoula public for what took place both at the bottom and the top of the building. Two stories below street level, tucked away down a puzzling maze of corridors, lay a smaller theater at whose box office Ed Sharp often personally presided. For decades, those of us who, entertaining visitors to Missoula, sought just the right way to convey to them the peculiar tenor of our local culture, would almost always include on the itinerary a visit to the Chapel of the Dove.

Seating no more than thirty customers for its standard fare of art films, the Chapel of the Dove was rarely remembered for what people had seen on its tiny screen. Framing that screen, the reverently presented life-size posters of Humphrey Bogart and Marilyn Monroe created for movie addicts the appropriate sense of silver screen sacredness. But here, Monroe and Bogart merely served as chorus for the main character, whose likeness appeared in various forms throughout the theater. Koro Hato, the white dove who lived for years in Ed Sharp's apartment upstairs, had greeted customers at the box office perched on Sharp's shoulder, or sometimes on the top of his head. And Koro's recorded lyrics to Sharp's organ accompaniment served as prelude to every Chapel of the Dove movie — Koro Hato was in fact The Dove to whose memory this theater had been dedicated.

Some there were who insisted, even (though never above a whisper) within the precincts of the chapel itself, that she was nothing more than a pigeon. Certainly the flock from which she descended — which still swooped and glided above Missoula's downtown and riverfront, always returning to the roof of the Wilma for the food Sharp provided them every day — certainly they were called "pigeons" by most of us most of the time. Now and then a downtown merchant, forced to line an already expensive storefront awning with netting to keep the birds from perching on its inner frame, might embellish the word "pigeon" a little, but mainly they were just called pigeons. Nevertheless, in the city's negotiations over the terms of its investment in the Wilma's renovation, when we got to the clause about how long after Ed Sharp's death the city would be obligated to continue feeding the birds, we always referred to them as "doves." As one old-timer put it, "Some things are not worth squabbling over."

When one of my constituents would ask me how the negotiations were going, I would usually refer, respectfully, to some of the special challenges that one faced in dealing with Mr. Sharp. In response, my questioner would typically smile and respectfully ask the standard one-word question, "Pigeons?" If there was any need for the conversation to go further, it might end with a reference to Mr. Sharp as "quite a character." Over the years, as one plan after another for the theater's restoration failed to come to fruition, I held many conversations with Ed Sharp about why his theater was so important to the city, and somewhere in the course of those conversations the word "character" fell into place for me in a suddenly obvious context. If Ed Sharp was a character, in any genuinely theatrical sense, then it was clear that the whole city was his stage. Whether it was the city parading past Eddie and Koro Hato at the Chapel's box office, or the city carrying on its business under the wheeling surveillance of Eddie's flock of "doves," Missoula was Ed Sharp's stage. As soon as I understood that, I began to pay attention in a new way to all the other "characters" I found myself dealing with around the city.

There were, as I could see once I took stock of the situation, quite a number of them. A few might and probably did qualify for official designation as mentally ill, and some of these were to be found among Missoula's homeless population, but not a few were, like Ed Sharp, people of some means, who had come by their wealth cleverly and persistently. Being a character was clearly not a class phenomenon, and as I tried to see what kind of phenomenon it was instead, I found it cutting across other lines as well. Before long, I realized that a very high percentage of the town's characters had established rather close, sometimes daily relations with the mayor. They seemed to take my attention for granted, and to assume that a certain familiarity existed between us even when I could not quite divine its source. Then it dawned on me that, for most of these people, the mayor was just one more character. Children's literature, with its ubiquitous portrayal of pompously ineffectual mayors, would have prepared them for this conclusion, but I came to sense that many of these people, by casting the mayor as a character, were also implicitly recognizing something important about the city itself. If the city, as so many of its most acute observers have concluded, is itself a form of theater, then of course its most visible official representative can only be a character.

At first I resisted this conclusion, insisting that I had been misapprehended, or at least miscast. But two factors worked to break down my resistance. First, I saw that the cast of the city's characters was actually many times larger than I had first reckoned it to be. As I paid closer attention to this category, I saw more and more people relating to the city through some distinctive set of characteristics, and that the ordered life of the city depended, to a certain extent, upon this being so. Many of us counted on others to stay more or less "in character." Some leeway is certainly permitted, some experimenting with roles even encouraged, but we depend in more ways than we might imagine on most of us staying in character most of the time.

These reflections helped wear down my resistance to admitting that the mayor was just one more character, and another line of thought finally won me over. It began when Oskar Schuster, mayor of Neckargemünd, first visited Missoula in a series of exchange visits which would culminate in Missoula and Neckargemünd becoming sister cities. Determined to give the Bürgermeister as much of the real flavor of Missoula as possible, we inevitably arranged to have him visit the Wilma, and especially the Chapel of the Dove. Attempting to prepare him for this adventure, we told him that we were giving him some clues to Missoula's character. We also warned him that we might run into Ed Sharp, whom we naturally described as "something of a character." Working hard on his English vocabulary, Mayor Schuster asked us whether Ed Sharp being a character had the same meaning as what we called the character of Missoula. I started to explain that here, once again, English was just making two unrelated words sound alike. But then it occurred to me that his un-English ear had caught a connection I had taught myself not to hear. Of course, Ed Sharp being the character he was had everything to do with Missoula's own character.

Eddie had not concocted his role out of thin air, any more than any of the rest of us do. Rather, we define and refine our roles in an ongoing dialogue between our personal stories and whatever the city gives us to work with. In the process (one that of course never ends), we weave our stories and our roles into one another and we play off one another in a way that is never the same from one place to another, giving each place a character of its own. Mayor Schuster had come to Missoula as part of a courtship that cities often conduct on the way to formalizing a sister city relationship, or what the Germans call a friendship. It amounts to nothing more or less than the two cities finding out whether they like each other well enough to commit to a lasting relationship. They cannot make such a decision unless they have some way of knowing who this other city is. In the end, nothing but local culture can answer that question.

Which is to say that local culture is one more way, one indispensable way, in which the wholeness of the city manifests itself. No life worth calling good is imaginable apart from the thousand subtle satisfactions such culture provides. But this is not culture as frosting, not something that can be added as an afterthought once all the basics of life are in place. Whether it is Dallas remembering its fascination with Pegasus, and then using that remembrance to begin the healing of a blighted downtown, or St. Louis asking how the design of a new arts and entertainment complex can best serve the needs and interests of the city's younger citizens, the kind of culture that sustains our humanness is the kind whose roots always mingle with the deep foundations of the city itself.

FOUR

The Health of Cities

The true city I believe to be the one we have described — the healthy city, as it were.

— PLATO, *The Republic*

J UST ANOTHER HUNDRED YARDS of this steep climb up
Whittaker Drive and I'll swing down onto High Park Way,
gear up, and begin the long glide back to the valley floor.
Every morning for several weeks I've added one more block to
my contest with this hill on Missoula's south side, using a
bicycle now to condition myself after back surgery ruled out
jogging as my main path to fitness. Gradually getting into
shape again after weeks of convalescence, I'm struck once
more by the inescapable interrelatedness of the body's various
systems. Muscles can't strengthen themselves very much unless heart and lungs expand their capacities as well. Faced in
midlife with elevated cholesterol levels, I've finally acknowledged that my arteries' capacity to supply a strengthening
muscular system depends in part on what I choose to eat. And
now the conditioning of my muscles has taken on an added
dimension, as I leave behind years of taking the skeletal system
for granted and begin to concentrate on developing those muscles whose job it is to help the spine do its work well, so that no
more errant disks will threaten the spinal cord as that lumbar
disk had so painfully done last January.

Even this early in my reconditioning campaign, the various pains and strains of the predawn ride pay dividends in terms of greater alertness and vitality later in the morning as I plunge into my biweekly, morning-long meeting in the mayor's conference room with my core management team. I've come to anticipate these meetings because of the untamed variety of topics appearing on the agenda. Ranging from how to launch a communitywide "Vision 2020" strategic planning process to the problem of delivery trucks blocking midmorning traffic on West Front Street, these meetings always remind me of how inescapably my job is hitched to the two-horse team of the ridiculous and the sublime. But always, in the crazy stew of these Tuesday agendas, I am struck by the relatedness of issues that at first sight seem utterly distinct.

This morning, enjoying the awareness of my slowly strengthening muscles, heart, and lungs, I muse about whether this connectedness of city issues is in any way similar to the relations among body systems I had encountered two hours earlier. How like a human body might the city be? As soon as the city attorney arrives, we will have to get to work on the agenda, but in the meantime I quickly scan it to see how many of its items are in some way related to issues of health. The answer is a little startling, but if I compare this agenda to any of the others we've worked through over the years, I see that the amount of attention we pay to issues of health is as steady as it is substantial.

As with the agenda at large, these items range wildly from the minute to the global, and they always present many subtle and unexpected linkages. Here are a few of the items on this morning's list:

* City Hall Smoking Policy
* Changes in the Employee Health Benefit Plan

* Agreement with the County to Establish a Water Quality District
* Rattlesnake Valley Trail Development
* Access to Health Care for the Medically Indigent
* Reducing Carbon Monoxide Emissions
* Relocation of City Bus Meet
* Closing Front Street for Western Montana Clinic Expansion
* Federal Grant for Drug Awareness Education

Not only do these issues bear, sometimes in bizarre ways, on each other, but as we discuss their intricacies, we often find ourselves tracing the history of a given issue back months, if not years, into the past, to roots that touch far more Missoula lives in far more textured ways than the dry agenda captions ever reveal. If the city were to be seen as an organism, the interwoven webs of these issues must be part of what makes it work, either well or poorly.

A year or so after that Tuesday morning, I began to learn something about a remarkable career that has turned upon just this intuition that cities are organisms, and that their own health is a prime determinant of the health of their inhabitants. Dr. Leonard Duhl, now living and working in Berkeley, California, grew up in New York City in a family which he describes as "full of doctors." His father, one of those doctors, "walked me around the city every weekend from the time I was four until I was fourteen, and in the process, taught me about most facets of city life."

Duhl, maintaining the family tradition, studied medicine, specializing in psychiatry, then took that training into a career in public health. From the beginning, Duhl seems to have maintained an integrated balance between the two primary influences on his early life: a love of the city in all its complexity, and a calling to the service of human health. As a public health official with special responsibility for issues of mental health, he began trying to persuade his colleagues that all the institutions that dealt with his clientele — courts, hospitals, welfare agencies, and others — should be thought of not as discrete entities with equally discrete missions to perform but as an integrated system. From the perspective of service delivery, this was a useful but hardly unique way of thinking about how to do a more efficient and effective job of helping people with mental health problems. But Duhl had something more in mind than making the bureaucracy more efficient.

All those walks with his father had taught him to think of the city as a system of intricately interrelated parts, and his medical training had given him the perfect bodily analogy to this way of seeing the city. So now, as he struggled with the overwhelming job of trying to stretch inadequate public resources across the human tragedy of mental illness, his instinct was to think of both his clients and the city itself in organic terms, trying to make the city more effective in combating mental illness by increasing the systemic integration of some of its own elements.

In the early sixties, Duhl took these perceptions to Washington, where his career continued to reflect his twin interests in cities and in health. Serving first as chief of planning for the Mental Health Institute in the Public Health Service and then as the special assistant to the secretary of housing and urban development, Duhl continued to argue that until cities were strengthened in a systemic, organic sense, no amount of federal aid, no number of federal programs would succeed in addressing the problems those programs sought to tackle. These arguments helped shape the Model Cities program, and to build an unprecedented level of public involvement in Lyndon Johnson's War on Poverty programs.

Duhl left the federal government in 1968, taking with him

to Berkeley his now even more firmly held belief in the relationship between the health or soundness of cities and the health of their inhabitants. His writing and teaching on the subject at the University of California led Duhl in 1984 to be invited to a conference in Toronto. Entitled "Beyond Health Care," the conference was designed to examine alternatives to society's increasing reliance on the health care industry as the primary way of securing human health. Dr. Duhl, drawing on his years of experience with both the Public Health Service and federal urban programs, suggested an alternative to the medical model. In his speech, "Let's Create Healthy Cities," he argued that a city was very much like an organism in which no part could be made healthy without attending to the health of all related parts. No amount of attention to improving the health care delivery system, then, would succeed unless the city itself was being strengthened in all its parts. A healthy physical environment, good housing, and a strong economy were as crucial to human health as good hospitals or medical insurance plans.

While many in his own profession received Duhl's argument with skepticism or even hostility, it fell on more fertile ground in other quarters. A short time after the Toronto conference, Duhl gave much the same speech to the World Health Organization. Desperate for some effective means of dealing with crushing health problems in all quarters of the globe, the WHO took up Dr. Duhl's call to create healthy cities as one of its chief objectives. Local communities began responding to this theme almost immediately; soon, networks of "healthy cities" had spread across Europe, Canada, and the United States. In this country, the National Civic League took on the work as one of its central missions.

Within a decade of Duhl's Toronto speech, some fifteen hundred cities around the world had established healthy cities programs. When Duhl organized a healthy cities conference in San Francisco in 1993, hundreds of these cities attended, and so did many that had never heard of the WHO or Civic League programs, but had, in the last few years, begun to operate on the same principles as those that informed the healthy cities movement. "Most of these cities thought they were alone in their efforts," Duhl recalls. "It was exciting to see them discovering how much they have in common and how much they could learn from each other."

What the healthy cities movement seems to be rediscovering is the age-old understanding that no individual citizen can be whole or healthy except as a member of a whole and healthy community. As Aristotle wrote, "Not being self-sufficient when they are isolated, all individuals are so many parts all equally depending on the whole which alone can bring self-sufficiency."[1] The reawakening of this ancient wisdom brings with it a memory of the meaning of "the body politic," encouraging us to imagine what a healthy political body might look like, and how it could sustain and complement the health or wholeness of individuals. This is the richly suggestive double meaning that seems to give so much force to the term "healthy city," evoking at once a city in which people are healthy and a city that is itself the political embodiment of health.

What reveals itself behind the double meaning of these words is not some neat trick of logic or rhetoric, but an infinitely complex, deeply human (and therefore never fully perfected) interplay between the wholeness or health of individuals and that of the cities within which they seek to live healthy lives. Dr. Duhl, for example, is convinced that, in straightforward physical terms, "the more connected people are with each other, the healthier they are. The more they are able to determine the conditions of their existence, the healthier they will be." Duhl is not speaking metaphorically; he is saying that a body politic that connects people to each other in ways that enable them to be self-determining is the surest context within which people might live healthy lives.

One of the unique contributions of the National Civic League to the healthy cities movement lies in the league's recognition of the connection between the nurturing of healthy cities and the development of a richer, more humanly satisfying kind of politics. Words like "collaboration" and "consensus" are sprinkled throughout the league's healthy cities literature. There are a number of compelling reasons for this emphasis. First, the fundamental premise of the healthy cities movement is that seemingly disparate arenas must be more fully integrated — so that those working for a reduction in teenage pregnancy, for example, need to be connected with those trying to strengthen the local economy. This requires a bridging of bureaucratic and other turf barriers. In almost every case, it requires people to question their preconceptions about one another's motivations or competencies.

Leonard Duhl equates this work with real politics. "The body politic," he says, "is simply the coming together of all the formerly fragmented players to find a common agenda." That is an almost exact description of how I experienced the issue that first led me to think about Missoula's place in the healthy cities movement. Scanning the agenda that Tuesday morning, my mind replayed several scenes in the "coming together of all the formerly fragmented players" that had constituted the evolution of the Missoula Partnership Health Center.

Like a young, growing tree, this issue had already developed a complex root system, of which the mayor's involvement was only a minor branch, reaching back to my first campaign for mayor. The Republican candidate for mayor in 1989 was the director of the Missoula Chamber of Commerce. Knowing that most hard-core business support would not be mine under those circumstances, but determined to build a strong base for governing if I should win, I met with several business leaders during the campaign in an effort to persuade them that I wanted their constructive involvement in my hoped-for administration, whether they supported my candidacy or not. As I made these rounds, I often asked which other business leaders I should visit, a question that brought my attention repeatedly to Larry White, the administrator of St. Patrick Hospital, one of Missoula's two major medical centers. I had been impressed by St. Patrick's aggressive involvement in a variety of civic affairs, and I hoped to learn from Larry White how we could strengthen the hospital's obvious commitment to active citizenship. Our first conversation persuaded me that Larry White was someone I would turn to frequently if I won the election.

Two years later, having worked on dozens of projects and initiatives with White and others on his staff, I asked him to talk about his involvement in one particular project: an innovative public and private response to the growing problem of medically uninsured Missoulians, those too poor to afford good insurance but not poor enough for Medicaid or old enough for Medicare. In the early nineties this problem became a central concern to many communities that, not knowing when or if a national health policy would emerge, had to address the problem as best they could locally.

St. Patrick Hospital had come to the issue of medical indigence from two directions at once. On the one hand, people who could not afford to go to doctors when they needed them often appeared in the hospital's emergency room, where they were certain to be taken care of even though there was often no chance that they could ever pay for the services they received there. This obviously created a financial problem for the hospital, as it does for most hospitals in most cities. In St. Patrick's case, the hospital's charitable mission brought an added dimension to bear on the issue. St. Patrick Hospital was established and is still operated by the Sisters of Providence, an order of Catholic nuns whose mission includes "a special concern for the marginalized and the poor." Larry White delights in citing the older Victorian formulation of this mission, in which the Sisters of Providence claimed a "prophetic solidarity with the poor." In either form, this is no empty motto for the Sisters of Providence, and as their professional administrator, Larry White understood that he was expected to bring this concern for the poor to life in the hospital's daily operations. Obviously, the growing problem of medical indigence fell squarely across the path of this mission.

The Missoula City-County Health Department had for years run an indigent clinic, which was now finding itself overcome by the growing caseload. Responding to this situation within the context of the charitable mission of his hospital, Larry White hired a recently retired physician, Dr. Hal Braun, to work at this public clinic, providing medical services to "the poor and the marginalized."

Dr. Braun is one of those smallish individuals whose energy and enthusiasm make you think that he might have started out much bigger, and had all his motive power compacted and intensified into a smaller frame. What got squeezed out, apparently, was any trace of laxness or disorderliness. Anyone who works with Dr. Braun for any length of time will soon understand that he knows exactly where he stands, and that before long he will expect the same of you. There is so little nonsense about the man that even the twinkle in his clear hazel eyes speaks less of levity than of a focused vitality. If anyone could help the indigent clinic get on top of its caseload, it would be someone with the energy of a Dr. Hal Braun.

But Dr. Braun's greatest contribution would not lie finally

in the number of patients he served, which could at best be a drop in an ever bigger bucket. What Larry White now congratulates himself for is not that he sent a workhorse to the clinic to serve the poor, but that he sent a "wise physician," who, in White's words, "could see the broader dimensions of the problem and help us find a solution to it." In this case, the broader dimensions included not only the fact that St. Pat's charitable contribution could only make a dent in the problem, but that the government was not going to solve it either. The federal government might someday address the issue of national health insurance, but in the early nineties, the signs of movement were not inspiring.

Meanwhile, Montana's state government had been caught for years in a partisan deadlock on fiscal matters, and as the red ink accumulated in Helena, the likelihood increased that state policies would only push more people into medical indigence. Local governments found themselves in a double bind. Since 1986, their property tax base had been frozen by a citizens' initiative, while the state legislature, which could have either lifted the cap or allowed local governments the option to expand their tax structure beyond property taxes, had instead allowed the statewide deadlock to strand local governments in a deepening fiscal quagmire.

It was in this climate that Dr. Hal Braun began working patiently toward a solution to Missoula's problem. From his work with the health department, and especially with its director, Ellen Leahy, he became convinced that local government by itself could not marshal enough resources to address the problem. He also saw that, in spite of its "prophetic solidarity with the poor," St. Patrick Hospital could not possibly hire enough Hal Brauns to meet this growing need. Braun found that the core of the problem was lack of access by the medically indigent to physicians, and that the physicians themselves must be part of the solution. When he first suggested this to the St. Patrick Hospital board of trustees, one of the members quipped that getting the doctors involved would make "prophetic solidarity with the poor" look like a piece of cake. "What we're going to need is a little prophetic solidarity with the rich," the trustee concluded.

The barriers to getting physicians to donate services extended beyond raw selfishness. While Dr. Braun knew that government could not supply the whole answer to this problem, he understood clearly that it had to be part of the solution. But he knew, and was soon painfully reminded, that relations between physicians and the local health department had often been strained. "The minute I began speaking with my colleagues about cooperating with the health department, that old mistrust came to the surface," he told me. "The first reaction of many physicians was to start rehashing old sins of the department, and reliving old battles with it."

If this were not discouraging enough, Braun was also reminded that even among the physicians themselves, the wounds of past battles had created a climate of deep cynicism about being able to address far simpler issues than the one he was now asking them to take on. "We'd become accustomed to a pattern of polarization over medical issues, where someone would struggle to get 51 percent of us to agree to some initiative, and then the 'winners' couldn't get anything done because the other 49 percent were so upset they'd do anything to stymie them." But over the years, in other settings, Dr. Braun had carefully observed and studied a different process: "Not starting with a solution and trying to get a majority to support it, but starting by agreeing on a statement of the problem, and then exploring ways of solving it."

When he puts it in this firm, manicured style, Dr. Braun

makes it sound simple. Discussions with other players in this drama leave no doubt, however, that Hal Braun's persistence and skill at getting people to listen to one another played a major role in the solution that began to emerge for this particular problem. That solution eventually came to be known as the Partnership Health Center — a true partnership of city and county government, the two Missoula hospitals, and dozens of local physicians. The center created a screening and referral system to provide a base level of health and medical services for a steadily expanding number of Missoula's medically indigent population. The program was innovative and promising enough to attract several major grants, and to help Ellen Leahy win national recognition for her role in it. None of it came easily, however.

All of the eventual partners in the project had originally presented Hal Braun with its own reasons not to become a full participant. Many of the doctors argued that this was government's problem, that instead of physicians donating services, each local government should just appropriate whatever was necessary to pay for the needed services. Dr. Braun knew that neither local government was in a position to do that, and to persuade his colleagues of this, he enlisted the help of Ellen Leahy. Trained as a nurse and chosen as the director of the health department on the strength of her managerial skills, Leahy could speak the physicians' language and bring them to accept the fact that public funds alone were not sufficient to address the problem.

Meanwhile, the local governments also brought some old wounds to the effort. My initial reaction, when Hal Braun visited my office to tell me that the city would soon be asked to contribute to the project, was to launch into a lecture about the awful condition in which state government had left city finances. Much as I might support what he was proposing, I let him know that there was next to no chance of his ever seeing Dollar One from the city treasury.

It is now difficult for me to imagine how I could so thoroughly have misjudged this visitor. He had not come to my office for a lecture on city finances or the evil ways of the state legislature, although he took it all in politely, even compassionately. What he had come for, and would keep coming back for until he got it, was what he asked for at the outset from each party he contacted: first, an acknowledgment that there was a medical indigence problem in Missoula, and second, a pledge to join a partnership of people intent on trying to solve it.

What finally secured my support for the partnership was a steadily deepening appreciation for the fragile coalition that Dr. Braun had forged. In all my years in politics, I had never heard of doctors and hospitals willing to make this kind of contribution to solving a social problem. It was clear to me that their remarkable yet still tentative commitment depended now upon some significant response and support from local government. Quite apart from the undeniable merits of the proposal, I concluded that the community could not afford to undermine this unprecedented consensus within the medical sector. Were we to refuse to participate now, no matter how sound our pleas of poverty, we would deepen still further the cynicism and mistrust that Dr. Braun and others had worked so hard to transcend.

In the spring of 1991, then, as I began preparing my executive budget, I included a $40,000 contribution to the Partnership Health Center, and guarded this particular new budget initiative through the painful paring of every other worthy new program. Each time my advisers suggested that we take a second look at that precious $40,000, I thought again of the hard-won commitment of the doctors and the hospital, finding myself confronted at each temptation by a sense of obligation to sustain that coalition.

Like any story line in the life of a city, this one never comes to a complete or perfect conclusion. Missoula, like every other American city, continues to be home to far too many uninsured or underinsured individuals and families. Therefore we are already at work on another, considerably bolder initiative to address this problem, and we carry into this next effort a margin of courage and confidence earned by working through the jealousies, bias, and mistrust that might easily have aborted the Partnership Health Center. Due to the patience and perseverance of people like Hal Braun, Ellen Leahy, and Larry White, dozens of Missoula families are healthier now than they would otherwise have been. But real health is rarely brought just to one part of the body, and that is as true of the body politic as it is of the human body. Somewhere in Missoula a woman who would not otherwise have had access to a mammogram has prevented the spread of an early cancer because now she could go to the doctor. And in the course of providing this type of access to medical care, we've also slowed if not reversed the spread of another malignancy: the deepening cynicism of health professionals about their own ability to cooperate with each other or with their local governments. This is a tentative cure, but we have made a beginning, and in the process gained enough trust and confidence to take the next step.

On this Tuesday morning, the issue facing my management team is no longer whether we will be part of the Partnership Health Center but how we will carry on its momentum. I can't help thinking that there is, in fact, a parallel to my hard ride up Whittaker Drive earlier that morning. A few weeks ago I couldn't have made it all the way up to High Park Way if my life depended on it, but through days of disciplined training, I earned the wide view of the Missoula Valley which was now mine each time I swung into my downhill glide. Two years ago, the ragged fabric of mistrust among local governments, doctors, and hospitals would have made a description of the partnership read like pure fiction, but now, after many painful steps against the limits of our endurance, we had become a different set of actors and, at least from my perspective, a healthier city.

On this morning's agenda, the question is whether our city government should join another partnership. We had been discussing with St. Patrick and community hospitals, with the doctors at Western Montana Clinic, and with the local school district the possibility of combining our employee health benefit plans. All of our organizations had developed self-insurance plans; now we explored the idea of pooling our programs and in the process creating the nucleus to which other large and then smaller employers might connect, with the goal of establishing a communitywide self-insurance program. This is easy to say, but nowhere nearly as easy to do.

Each of the participants had devised its own governing structure for its self-insurance program; most (like ours at city hall) included committees of employees who cared deeply about the package of benefits they had negotiated, and who would view with instant suspicion any tampering with their program. In addition, all the organizations had governing bodies that, like the city council in my case, would have to be persuaded to lower the turf barriers and allow other partners some control over what had previously lain exclusively within our organization's domain. But more than once, as we struggled with what sometimes seemed insurmountable technical obstacles, I saw how the earlier success of so many of these players in forging the Partnership Health Center sustained them in facing these new challenges, giving them confidence that what seemed insurmountable might, with intelligent determination and goodwill, be overcome.

It was the recurrence of goodwill, at so many crucial points in the process, that kept us moving forward. As I observed how important that goodwill had become, I realized how crucial will itself was to our forward movement. I thought of my predawn bicycle rides, during which will alone had added another leg to each morning's climb. I thought of Hal Braun's persistence in piecing together the Partnership Health Center, and I questioned what was driving this new effort against great odds. What I saw was an indispensable exercise of will by all the players, and I became especially interested in the motives (the willed movement) of the hospitals. As I watched their determination to make this thing happen, and as I simultaneously learned more about the healthy cities movement, I was struck by what seemed something of a paradox.

In city after city, the starting point for the healthy cities movement is that which brought Leonard Duhl to Toronto and would later make the World Health Organization so ready for his message: the recognition that our heavy reliance upon a "health care delivery system" is not adequately serving the needs of human health. Referring to this inadequacy, the National Civic League's Tyler Norris suggests what seems at first glance a surprising alternative:

> With such limitations to the medical model, the emphasis is shifting to a broader model of health that reflects a deeper understanding of the determinants of health — environmental, social, political, behavioral, biological, and medical. Additionally, given the scope and complexity of health, and the facets of the community that affect health,

the various sectors of the community must all be involved in the process of supporting healthy people and creating a Healthy Community.[2]

Over and over within the lore and literature of this movement, we find healing and wholeness being advanced in one breath. Tyler Norris argues that "Healthy cities are represented by leadership that focuses on the whole of a city and can visualize both parts and 'wholes' simultaneously." "Health crosscuts everyone, regardless of race or class," Norris says. "It builds off assets, not needs and shortcomings. It builds on what is already working."

Instead of concentrating solely on reforms in the health care delivery system, then, communities involved in this movement stress unlikely subjects like "a sense of history to which their citizens relate and upon which their commonly held values are grounded," or "a complex and interactive economy." They highlight how disparate features of a good city like affordable housing, trail systems, urban design, open space, air quality, and employment opportunities can be fit together to enhance the health of citizens far more effectively and cheaply than the traditional reliance on the health care delivery system. "The overall quality of life is a far more important determinant of human health than is the quantity or even the quality of medical care," Leonard Duhl argues. "Medical care accounts for perhaps 10 percent of what makes people healthy. The other 90 percent depends on the community's health."

Thus, for example, when Pasadena, California, found itself deadlocked in land-use debates, the effort to turn those debates into an exercise in constructive citizenship evolved into the "Pasadena 2000" visioning process, which the city highlighted as a key element of its healthy cities initiative. In Seattle, Kids-Place was also held up as healthy cities work, even though, like Pasadena 2000, it had nothing to do with the health care delivery system.

Yet very often, hospitals and medical centers also play a key role in their communities' healthy cities initiatives. What accounts for the fact that health care professionals so often take the lead in a movement that openly questions our reliance on the health care delivery system? Motivated, it seems, by the often cataclysmic uncertainty of the future of their industry in the context of national policy, wise hospital administrators like Larry White have become alert to the possibilities of establishing a more secure framework closer to home. Recognizing that the amount of money any given locality can afford to spend on health care must be limited, leaders in the field think in terms of how to keep the whole community healthy with that finite pool of resources. This inevitably leads to Duhl's point: the community's health is the most cost-effective place to invest in individual health. So, in the most unexpected way, as medical centers seek to clarify their own identity, they are drawn more and more deeply into citizenship, one result of which is that they help bring their cities to a clearer understanding of their own organic nature and of their own need for health and wholeness.

In Utica, New York, St. Elizabeth's Hospital and the Loretto Geriatric Center, both located in the very poor Cornhill neighborhood, have worked with the city government and the neighborhood to develop a job training, neighborhood leadership, and urban youth citizens corps program "to breathe life back into this area," which the partners describe as "the most distressed neighborhood in a generally distressed city." Together, they plan to convert an old school in the neighborhood into a $22-million health care and community center, using it among other things to provide job training and employment opportunities in the health care field for the neighborhood's young people. In what is becoming the standard approach in such undertakings, the city and the medical centers have seen to it that "all of the major individuals and organizations who provide services within Cornhill have achieved consensus on goals and objectives for the revitalization effort." In a classic statement of the principle that the healing of one part of a city can lead to the healing of others, the partners in the Cornhill project have set themselves the goal of making this "a model in other distressed areas" in and around Utica.

In Portland, Oregon, Emanuel Hospital and Health Center, also located in a depressed area, has taken stock of the fact that even though the hospital is situated in a residential neighborhood, very few of its employees live there, instead commuting great distances. So Emanuel has become a major player in a neighborhood revitalization program, aimed at assisting its employees in buying and rehabilitating houses in the area, thereby improving those employees' well-being and productivity, and in the process improving the neighborhood itself.

In Arkansas, the Fort Smith Health Alliance grew out of an effort by the chamber of commerce to slow the rapidly increasing cost of health care. While at first there was considerable tension between businesses (as consumers of health care) and hospitals (as health care providers), the tension was resolved as businesses responded to the hospitals' genuine desire to redefine their own role within the community. The hospitals, whose operations were already regional, helped the alliance focus on the larger city-region as its natural domain, rather than solely on Fort Smith. That regional perspective was especially challenging in this case, because the city-region reaches across the Arkansas border to serve 120,000 Oklahoma residents.

In South Bend, Indiana, the chamber of commerce was also

the convener of the healthy cities initiative, again in an effort to lower health care costs. As in Fort Smith, the city's four hospitals were troubled by an effort to reduce hospital revenues. Memorial Hospital and Health Center, the largest of the community's hospitals, was, like so many other medical centers, in the midst of rethinking its own mission. And like many another progressive medical center across the country, Memorial had invited the hospital guru Leland Kaiser to help in the effort. Now, confronted by the chamber of commerce's initiative, Memorial invited Kaiser back to South Bend to work, not just with the hospital, but with three hundred citizens from across the community.

Using the National Civic League's healthy communities model, this broad cross section of community leaders produced eleven initiatives that they agreed to pursue for the improvement of South Bend's quality of life. One of the initiatives was the creation of a Center for Collaboration, to teach people how to communicate across the various lines that divide the community. Here Memorial Hospital provided a classic case of a "health care provider"; in the course of reassessing its own mission, it came to see the community's health as central to that mission. "When you go through the healthy cities process, you assess the civic health of the community," Memorial's Carl Ellison said. "You ask, 'Are groups really talking to each other? If not, why not?'"

Carl Ellison, Memorial Hospital's assistant vice president for community affairs, is an African-American, and he is concerned that "this healthy cities process can seem rather hollow to people who are least advantaged." But Ellison's faith in the process runs deep, and he is convinced that even though "the work might take a generation," it is worth the effort and the patience. "The beauty of the process is that it will, absolutely, create new allies among people who have never before known how to work together," Ellison says. He offers one small but potent example.

South Bend's healthy cities steering committee included two men, Mike Mather and John Cohoat, who had never met, and who began the process with very little use for each other. Mather was the pastor of the Broadway Christian Parish, serving a neighborhood that was 50 percent black, 40 percent white, and 10 percent Hispanic. Cohoat was the president of Bonnie Doon Ice Cream, which had recently closed an ice cream parlor in the neighborhood because of vandalism. As the discussions about various aspects of South Bend's health progressed, Pastor Mather finally brought himself to ask Cohoat, "Why don't you reopen that Bonnie Doon and hire kids from the neighborhood to work in it? You might not have so much vandalism that way, and it would improve things in the neighborhood by providing more jobs and a place for kids to go in the bargain."

Carl Ellison enjoys telling this story, because Mather and Cohoat made it work. "That happened because we gave them an opportunity to talk, which they would never have had otherwise," Ellison recounts. "There aren't that many opportunities in South Bend for people like Mike and John to focus positively on the future." And behind that opportunity, Ellison knows, lies the farsighted thinking of an institution like Memorial Hospital and Health Center, which in turn contributed to a city's new way of thinking about community problems. "That Bonnie Doon reopened because South Bend made community the forethought and the afterthought," Ellison concluded. "It was not a hospital doing to the community; it was the community learning to take care of itself."

In Detroit, the community's path to that outcome carried a special twist. The Greater Detroit Area Health Council, along

with the mayor's office, convened a large number of stakeholders — business, labor, hospitals, insurers, government,
and consumers — for a "Healthy Detroit" initiative. All of the
stakeholders were asked to list and prioritize their particular
interests in such an effort. The first choices were all over the
map: hospitals wanted fewer uninsured drop-ins; unions
wanted their negotiated health plans protected, and so on. No
two first priorities coincided, but without exception, every
stakeholder listed as a second priority improving the health
status of Detroit citizens. The overwhelming consensus on this
objective guaranteed that all parties would ask themselves
what they could do, individually and collectively, to help Detroit citizens become more healthy.

But here again, the health of the city itself had been established as an inescapable background to the effort to improve
individual health. As in Fort Smith and South Bend, the chamber of commerce had been involved in the healthy cities initiative from the outset. In Detroit's case, the chamber's involvement had begun when business leaders had invited David
Rusk, former mayor of Albuquerque and author of *Cities Without Suburbs*, to a chamber retreat. Rusk argued, as he does
consistently, that cities like Detroit, whose suburbs were ignoring the plight of the central city, were losing competitiveness
compared to cities with more integration (of every kind) between city and suburbs. "People were very upset at that message," recalls Jim Kenney, president of the Greater Detroit
Area Health Council. "But then, almost immediately, Mayor
Archer was elected and began saying the same thing." Archer
was also, as Kenney says, "An outstanding, enthusiastic mayor
with the vision to see how both the city-state and the healthy
cities movements fit in with his desire to revitalize the city."
Without that vision, the diverse stakeholders may never have
stayed in one room long enough to find that behind their

wildly diverse top priorities lay a unifying desire to improve the health of citizens in Detroit. Once again, it was the discovery of a shared commitment to the community's civic health that enabled the city to begin to address in a serious and fruitful way the health of its citizens.

This interweaving of concern for individual health and for civic health also lay at the heart of Orlando's healthy cities initiative. Sharon McLearn, the director of community partnerships for the six-hospital Orlando Regional Healthcare System, attended the National Civic League's healthy cities training session on the advice of South Bend's Carl Ellison. Here again, the medical center had changed its mission from health care delivery to improving Orlando's quality of life. McLearn came back from the Civic League's training session determined that this new mission "would reach beyond smoking cessation classes and aerobics." McLearn wanted the Regional Healthcare System to take its new mission seriously enough to work on issues such as crime and homelessness. But as a relative newcomer to Orlando, she was not sure whether that could happen or not.

McLearn soon found herself allied with someone who was not by any means a newcomer to Orlando. Following up on her healthy cities training, she asked her board of directors to establish a community benefits committee. The board complied, and asked one of its own, Marilyn King, to chair the committee. King knew Orlando front to back and inside out. "If it happened in Orlando, Marilyn was involved," McLearn says. "But she also felt that there had to be a better way for Orlando to do things, because too many civic efforts had failed." King was fascinated by McLearn's account of the healthy cities movement, and decided to use it as a way to get beyond the all-too-frequent blocks to Orlando's community efforts.

McLearn and King's first effort to get community leaders together was also a failure. "It was a total bomb," McLearn moans. "We were mortified. Most of the people said, 'We don't need some fancy Civic League ideas; let's just do something.'" But King had had enough of "just do it" civics, and McLearn was still convinced that the health of cities was a powerful idea, capable of making a difference in Orlando. Assisted by two other farsighted women, the mayor of Orlando and the chair of the Board of County Commissioners, King and McLearn convened some one hundred and fifty broadly diverse stakeholders from throughout the community, who together began to articulate visions for Orlando. At the top of their list appeared a cluster of issues all relating to respect, tolerance, trust, and community connectedness. The stakeholders committed themselves to improving Orlando's civic health by pursuing these priorities.

There are almost certain to be other setbacks in this process, like the one that unsettled Sharon McLearn and Marilyn King early on. But the very determination to carry a strong vision through such setbacks is itself a healing act within the community, and like the Bonnie Doon story in South Bend, it will lead inevitably to larger acts of healing.

What this all seems to amount to is a different approach to healing than the health delivery system has typically pursued. Medical institutions in hundreds of cities find themselves motivated to reexamine and put a sounder footing on their relationship to their clientele, to their neighborhoods, to their regions, and to their employees. As medical centers build stronger workplaces, healthier neighborhoods, and a more sustainable relationship with their patients, new meaning attaches to the old injunction "Physician, heal thyself!" What Larry White's "wise physician" recognizes is that no doctor, no hospital, can secure its own health in isolation. So it happens that, in the process of redefining and resituating themselves, hospitals and medical centers everywhere are contributing in crucial ways to the healing, the making more whole, of their cities. Hospitals alone cannot accomplish this, just as neighborhoods alone cannot revitalize themselves; youth employment programs cannot succeed alone, just as muscles alone cannot become stronger without the strengthening of the heart and lungs. But hundreds of cities are now learning, by pulling together, by building upon yesterday's strengthening disciplines, how the body politic might slowly be restored to greater health.

FIVE

Focusing the Countryside

A low haze hangs on the houses
— firewood smoke and mist —
Slanting far to the Kamo river
and the distant Uji hills.
Farmwomen lead down carts
loaded with long white radish;
I pack my bike with books —
all roads descend toward town.

—GARY SNYDER,
"Work to Do toward Town"

W E LIKE HISTORY to accommodate our sense of order and proportion by dividing itself into neatly identifiable centuries. While it rarely succeeds in placing its corner-turning events squarely on years ending with several zeroes, history does sometimes provide us with usable centuries roughly corresponding to our numerology. The nineteenth century, for example, as a historically meaningful era, is now generally said to have occupied the years and events between Napoleon's defeat at Waterloo in 1815 and the Archduke Ferdinand's assassination in Sarajevo in 1914.

By that accounting, the twentieth century may prove to be short in years, if not in tumult. If it began with the world's descent into a series of bloody global conflicts, it may well have ended in 1989 in Berlin, Prague, Gdansk, and Moscow with the almost eerily peaceful conclusion of the cold war. But if we were to insist that history provide us with an event closer to the year 2000 to mark the turn of this century, we might well look to Hong Kong's long-planned departure from the British Empire in 1997. That event may teach us, as nothing else has yet done, of the power of cities and city economies to remake the world and its history.

Forced into the empire in 1842 at the height of the opium war, Hong Kong had served as a strategic British outpost until its capture by the Japanese during the Second World War. Restored to the empire in 1945, the city soon assumed a new geopolitical significance when, with Mao Tse Tung's communist victory on mainland China, Hong Kong became, along with Taiwan, a refuge for those most intensely motivated to escape the communist regime. It was against the background of the cold war's East-West struggle that Hong Kong's fate was most often viewed, especially after 1984, when Britain negotiated with Beijing an agreement to return Hong Kong to China in 1997. But in fact Hong Kong had prepared itself to play a very different role in history, one having far less to do with the struggle between communism and capitalism than with the place of cities in the political order. If 1997 proves to be more than a blip on the chart of history, it will be because Hong Kong's transition marks, more strongly than any other single event, the end of the age of the nation-state and the refocusing of human affairs around an almost forgotten yet irrepressible alternative: the city-state.

In the era of the nation-state, we came to take for granted those maps of the world on which every single bit of land mass (except Antarctica) was assigned a color corresponding to the nation claiming sovereignty over it. So, with Hong Kong, it was assumed that the new maps produced in 1997 would simply change the city's coloration from, say, the green of the Commonwealth to the orange of the People's Republic. But, long before 1997, Hong Kong had itself irretrievably redrawn the real, living map of its part of the world. It had done so simply by succeeding as a city. Its remarkable economic success had, like a powerful magnet, etched its lines of force into the surrounding countryside, as if oblivious to the fact that many of those surroundings were still part of the People's Republic. By 1990, Beijing had already granted to Guangzhou Province the right to operate as a "special economic zone," enabling this region to carry capitalism much further forward than any other part of the People's Republic. What this amounted to was simply a recognition by the Beijing government that it would be to everyone's advantage to allow Hong Kong to exercise its natural economic influence within its own region.

Once that influence was acknowledged, there was little chance of a reversal. China's need for foreign currency would not be diminishing after 1997, and long before then it had become clear that Hong Kong could generate far more of that currency if its natural economic relationship to its surrounding region were given the freest possible rein. Reduced to its simplest terms, what all this meant was that the historical logic of the city-state had become more compelling than the logic of the nation-state. To understand the historical significance of 1997, then, we need to consider in more general terms why the predominance of the nation-state in the modern era has begun to give way to the postmodern rebirth of the city-state.

After decades of observing cities more closely than any other American journalist of his generation, Neal Peirce finally concluded that as the economy had become more global, nations had steadily lost their economic relevance. "Nation-states," Peirce wrote, "excel at war; they are proving increasingly limited and sometimes shockingly incompetent in the arena of economics."[1] But the very globalization of the economy that had weakened nationhood from without was at the same time strengthening another, internal challenge to nationhood. The new configuration of the global economy, Peirce wrote, "drives one to visualize our great cities, their suburbs, exurbs, and geographic realms of influence as *citistates* — entities that perform as critical actors, more on their own in the world economy than anyone would have dreamed since the birth of the nation-state in the sixteenth and seventeenth centuries."[2]

Peirce's book, *Citistates,* was written after the fall of communism had opened the door to a "new world order" which would see more challenges to established nationhood in five years than had been witnessed in the preceding fifty. But well before Berlin tore down the wall that had sundered its cityhood, Jane Jacobs had prophetically sounded the two themes that Peirce now made the basis of his city-state argument. Like Peirce, Jacobs saw that the essence of nationhood had always had more to do with war and defense than with the creative, productive, entrepreneurial work of economies. Convinced that city regions alone produced prosperity while nations pursued a very different mission, Jacobs foresaw that the outcome of the struggle between the Soviet and the American empires would center upon their mutual effort to spend each other (mainly through the arms race) into oblivion or submission. "Today," she wrote in 1984, "the Soviet Union and the United States each predicts and anticipates the economic decline of the other. Neither will be disappointed."[3]

Having apparently won the cold war, Americans may be tempted to say that the Soviet Union's capitulation reflects its economic decline and our ascendancy. But that viewpoint requires us to ignore the overwhelming national debt we incurred in the course of the war, both the domestic debt of government borrowing and the international debt brought about by years of radical imbalance between imports and exports. The huge backlog of social problems, ranging through crime and drugs, homelessness, welfare, and health care, is one more form of indebtedness incurred in our single-minded pursuit of national ascendancy. Now, with the cold war behind us, our inclination is to address these issues with new national policies and programs. But if Peirce and Jacobs are right, the nation is likely to prove as inefficient and ineffective in this arena as it ever has been.

To the extent that the solution of social problems depends upon the sustained and sustainable generation of prosperity, the time has arrived to acknowledge that the nation-state is bankrupt — literally broke in terms of its multiple and crushing debts — but also bankrupt in terms of its capacity either to generate or to effectively reinvest the prosperity required to address the problems it continues to treat as its obligation and domain. "But if national governments are losing their power to innovate, to reposture a society," Peirce asks, "who will? To us [Peirce and his researchers], the inescapable conclusion is that the citistates have the potential to tackle these challenges."[4]

Why might cities, or "city-states," prove to be more capable than nations of generating prosperity or of deploying that prosperity to address social problems? The answer is necessarily complex, but behind any extended argument for the economic or social efficacy of the city lies the simple fact that a city is by its nature organic, and that it bears to its surrounding region an organic relationship that is the very essence of a successful economy. Unless we understand the compelling power of these natural organisms, we will be repeatedly astounded by their ability to wear down and render irrelevant national and other artificial boundaries — and we will there-

fore fail to appreciate or to assist the transition from the age of
the nation-state to the new global age of the city-state. But with
or without our conscious assistance, city economies will continue, relentlessly, to remake the world.

Phrases like "a successful economy" and "a growing economy" roll so easily from our tongues, pens, and keyboards that
we no longer pay much attention to what they really mean, or
what it might take for them to mean anything at all. To speak of
"an economy" implies that there must be more than one, and
that each has an identity, a shape, and boundaries of its own.
However, our language soon betrays a remarkable mental lazi-
ness on this score. No day passes, for example, without some
Montana official speaking about "the Montana economy."
Who can seriously believe that something as vital and fluid as
"an economy" could be contained or in any significant sense
defined by a set of arbitrarily drawn straight lines across the
landscape, lines crossing the Continental Divide, encompass-
ing on one side millions of acres of arid grassland and on the
other more millions of acres of timber and mountain valleys?
The economic activity generated by these landscapes cannot
possibly be improved by imposing upon it artificial boundaries
like those of state lines, or artificial names like "the Montana
economy." The economic activity generated by such landscapes might, however, be intensified and turned to greater
human purpose by closely heeding how it, and how the landscape, define in their own terms something that can meaning-
fully be called "economies." In every case, such real economies
turn out to be nothing other than the organic relationship of
cities and towns to their surroundings.

It is almost impossible to describe these relationships without sooner or later resorting to the image of a nucleus within a
larger structure. Sometimes the larger structure looks like a
living cell, sometimes more like an atom, but from either per-

spective, the city supplies the function of a nucleus for an organized set of entities and activities surrounding it. Like a cell or an atom, a city region is a distinct, meaningful, indeed indispensable structure of wholeness, without which (at least from the perspective of human beings) the world itself would lose all coherence. And like a cell or an atom, the city region depends for its coherence upon its nucleus, without which it can neither exist nor function.

I always enjoy flying home to Missoula, beginning to recognize once again familiar landscape after traveling to places I have not seen before, anticipating the multitude of ways in which the city will soon again engage my attention and energy. I also enjoy flying into Missoula, or any other city, because of the opportunity it provides to observe the intensifying level of activity that appears as the plane nears the city. From scattered farmsteads and villages, the network of highways, rail lines, and power lines begins to converge as the density of dwellings and other buildings steadily increases. Finally, if the city is a large one, the skyline of the central business district will appear, proclaiming dramatically that here activity is so concentrated that it cannot be contained at ground level, but has been pushed into the sky itself.

Nothing is so fundamental to a city as the concentration of humans and human activity within a small compass. All the problems that we call urban problems derive from this compactness, but we remain willing to struggle with them because of some constellation of human goods that seems unattainable except by means of such concentration. In fact, from the earliest institution of the marketplace, the gathering of humans and human activity in one place has remained crucial to the functioning of economies. Here the image of the nucleus becomes more than a metaphor as we see how the city market, by accumulating in one spot a critical mass of human energy and activity, creates in a very nearly physical sense a gravitational field whose lines of force expand the vitality of the center while simultaneously reaching into and organizing the surrounding countryside. It is precisely the synergy created by this concentration of human activity that makes the city the fundamental engine of all economic growth and change. When such engines assume the proportions of a Hong Kong, they can affect events on a global scale. But very small towns can also help us understand how the creative synergy of concentration operates to make economies work.

For years, my favorite local example of such synergy has been provided by the small ranching community of Drummond, fifty miles upriver from Missoula, where Flint Creek, descending from the snowcapped Pintlar Range, flows into the Clark Fork River. The Flint Creek and Clark Fork valley bottoms provide excellent winter pastures and hay meadows, supplementing the higher summer pastures in the surrounding mountains and more or less guaranteeing that Drummond's economy would center around cattle ranching. However, any observant visitor to the Drummond area will notice that the animals grazing these pastures are not just cattle in general, but that most are bulls, raised to be sold as breeding sires to ranches throughout the Northern Rockies.

Raising bulls is a very specialized form of ranching, requiring everything from expert knowledge of feed grains and hay to exceptionally sturdy fences for containing the sometimes explosive energy of bovine masculinity. Because buying a good bull is such a crucial choice for any rancher, most buyers want to be able to inspect their choices carefully, and to have a suitable range of sires to choose among. This adds up to a need for one single place in which a number of bulls can be shown and auctioned, and here again the heft and feistiness of these animals means that normal standards for sales ring or loading chute construction will not suffice. No single rancher could supply enough bulls or an adequate auction ring to make such a market work, but in Drummond, the combination of landscape, climate, and entrepreneurship created over several decades a synergy that gradually converted more and more of the surrounding ranches to this specialized purpose and eventually turned Drummond into the center of the region's breeding bull market.

This little economy could not exist or be sustained without Drummond as its nucleus. The market itself — in this case the auction ring and adjoining railhead — is the cornerstone of the economy. Less obvious but probably no less crucial is the role of the Wagon Wheel Cafe in bringing a number of ranchers together for coffee, lies, and gossip every morning. No one morning's storytelling would be likely to stand out as a turning point in the industry, but there is little room for doubt that over the course of many such mornings, the minutiae of skills and wisdom peculiar to bull-raising have circulated, competed, triumphed, or been vanquished, and finally have woven themselves more tightly together into that synergy that has earned Drummond the title "The Bullshippers' Capital of the World."

Meanwhile, downriver in Missoula, a different kind and level of synergy had been evolving. After decades of relying on timber cutting and sawmill production as the base of its economy, Missoula began to read on the wall the handwriting that was eventually to transform economic reality throughout the Northern Rockies and the Pacific Northwest, as a convergence of overcutting and heightened environmental awareness sharply curtailed the supply of timber to the region's sawmills. As a number of sawmills closed in and around Missoula in the seventies and eighties, local business leaders began looking for ways to shore up what appeared to be a shrinking if not disintegrating economic base. After an early round of clumsy, often painful and divisive efforts at industrial recruiting, the Missoula Economic Development Corporation began paying closer attention to what was actually happening within the Missoula economy, as a means of understanding how it might most effectively work to strengthen that economy.

The group learned that alongside the still very substantial lumber-producing industry, pockets, or "clusters," of other types of businesses had developed over the years. Missoula's two major hospitals, for example, along with the University of Montana, had begun serving as centers around which a number of biomedical research and development enterprises had clustered. The number of writers and artists living in and around Missoula had grown steadily over the years, and with that increase came more galleries, small publishers, and organizations offering workshops and retreats for artists and writers from throughout the West. Missoula had established a reputation as a bicycle-friendly city, and related to this, partly as cause, partly as consequence, two national bicycle organizations, one devoted to bicycle touring and the other to bicycle safety, had located their headquarters in Missoula, employing between them several dozen people.

As the Missoula Economic Development Corporation gained a clearer understanding of this clustering and the role of its synergy in the expansion of Missoula's economy, it used this knowledge to attract more employers to Missoula. We used this insight, for example, when we learned that the Boone and Crockett Club, the exclusive trophy-hunting organization founded by Teddy Roosevelt, was moving its national headquarters from the Washington, D.C., area to a western location. Once Missoula found itself on the club's short list of possible destinations, we fed the club's officers information about the growing number of similar activities already located in Missoula.

Boone and Crockett's decision to relocate arose in the context of its own redefinition of its mission, especially its growing understanding that its old function of keeping careful records of prize trophies had been gradually overshadowed by its work on protection of habitat for the animals it had previously seen only as prey. If the club was going to increasingly devote itself to habitat preservation, it made sense for its central office to be near such habitat. And it made sense (or so we argued) for its headquarters to be located in a city that was at once surrounded by such habitat and increasingly busy with a variety of activities concerned with preservation and enhancement of that habitat.

The work of the University of Montana's School of Forestry on habitat issues had already led the Boone and Crockett Club to endow a chair in that field at the Forestry School. But were the club's officers aware that the Rocky Mountain Elk Foundation, devoted to the protection of elk habitat, had already relocated its national headquarters to Missoula, or that Region One of the National Forest Service had long been headquartered in Missoula? We recounted how, every spring, the International Wildlife Film Festival brought wildlife filmmakers from all quarters of the globe to Missoula for juried showings of the best new films about wild animals. All this, we argued, created a fertile cluster of actors and activities within which the newly defined mission of the Boone and Crockett Club would be very much at home.

But if Missoula had made its way onto the club's short list of possible new homes, it was not alone on that list, and as the club's decision neared, the competition escalated. We began to hear of efforts by some of our competitors to raise doubts about Missoula's suitability as the organization's headquarters. "Yes, Missoula is home to all those groups and activities it brags about, but Boone and Crockett is still a hunting organization;

hunting is becoming more controversial, and Missoula seems to thrive on and breed such controversy," one argument ran. "We've heard that Missoula is also home to a number of anti-hunting activists and groups. Do you really want to run the risk of their picketing your board of directors' meetings?"

The club's response to these cautionary arguments, as it was reported to me, confirmed my growing conviction that the synergy of closely related activities lay somehow at the heart of economic vitality. "Yes," the club said, in effect, "we are a hunting organization, but that now means that we have to be a conservation organization. Conservation is challenging work; no one has all the answers about how best to do it, and we think sound and sustainable answers are more likely to come from vigorous debates among committed practitioners than from isolated efforts of people or organizations who think they already know the answers." And with that, the club called the mayor's office to say that it had decided to move its headquarters to Missoula.

By itself, this decision would not make or break the Missoula economy; it would probably not even have a statistically significant impact on it. But for me, the episode was most important because of what it enabled us to understand about how the city functions as an organic economy, and how that economy necessarily depends upon and shapes the equally organic relationship between Missoula and its surroundings.

If the Economic Development Corporation had been asked to give a name to its efforts to persuade the Boone and Crockett Club to move to Missoula, it would probably have said "business recruitment." As a nonprofit organization, though, the club does not fit into the category of what we usually call "a business," and in fact there are those who have argued that only private, for-profit enterprises should count as instances of successful business recruitment. On the other hand, nonprofit organizations such as the Rocky Mountain Elk Foundation or Bikecentennial can become major employers in the local economy, so it would seem shortsighted to exclude them from consideration for "business recruitment."

Beyond their contribution to the job base, such organizations and activities, when they begin to show signs of clustering and synergy, invite us to think about business itself in a more fundamental sense. The word "business" has taken on such a specialized meaning in our profit-oriented society that we have almost wholly forgotten its original meaning. But as soon as we recall that business simply means busy-ness, we at once bring into sharper focus the crucial role of cities in economic activity. Busy-ness is almost by definition a function of human concentration. We can, it is true, think or speak of an individual being "busy," but what we really mean is that the individual is creating a flurry of activity by bringing a number of her faculties to bear around a single enterprise. The notion of busy-ness is therefore much more likely to call to mind a beehive or an anthill — those quintessentially social settings where the concentration of individuals induces a constantly creative and restorative activity. The synergy produced by such concentrated busy-ness is of the very essence of cities, and is also the heartbeat of economies.

In fact, if we move up the organic scale from the cell to a complex organism, the image of the city as nucleus might shift to that of the city as the regional economy's heart, as it continually draws goods, capital, information, and people into itself by those highways, rails, and transmission lines we see converging on it as we fly in — drawing them in, mingling and enriching them by all the forms of its busy-ness — and then pumping them out again in a never-ending interchange between city and countryside which, the more closely we attend, the more we recognize as something that might in fact be called "an economy."

As more groups discover Missoula's synergistic clustering around issues of habitat and ecosystem, they examine more closely the relationship between Missoula and the ten-thousand-or-so-square-mile region for which it serves in so many ways as the nucleus. Like the Boone and Crockett Club, other organizations have come to this new way of understanding what Missoula is all about in the course of reexamining their own role in a changing world. The Forest Service offers what for me has been an intriguing example of this interlocking evolution of the city and its major economic components.

Located in the heart of the timber-producing reaches of the Northern Rockies, Missoula was destined to be a timber town, and with the late-nineteenth-century addition of the University of Montana and especially its School of Forestry to the city, it perhaps became inevitable that not only would sawmills, plywood plants, and a paper mill be located in Missoula, but that the federal agency responsible for managing those millions of acres of trees would also have a major presence here. When the Forest Service established its system of regions and regional headquarters around the country, Missoula became one of those headquarters, taking special pride, of course, in the fact that this was not just any region, but Region One. Both the Forest Service Smokejumper Center and the national Intermountain Fire Sciences Laboratory are also located in Missoula. All this Forest Service presence testifies to the extent to which Missoula's economy throughout most of this century has centered around trees, and especially around the cutting of trees.

That era has rather abruptly ended, not only in Missoula, but throughout the Pacific Northwest. Its final chapter coincided with the sobering retrenchment of the federal government which so characterized the Reagan-Bush era, continuing into the Clinton-Gore administration with the recognition that the time borrowed for so many decades with borrowed money has run out, that the federal government must learn to live in real time on real money, and that there is no way to make that transition except by a substantial rethinking of the role of agencies like the Forest Service. So just as the sustainability of the northern forests has come under searing scrutiny, the Forest Service has had to turn that same scrutiny on its own mission and its own methods.

One major product of that reexamination has been a shift in the Forest Service's emphasis from commodity production to what it calls "ecosystem management." Having settled upon that phrase, the agency at once found itself embroiled in an internal debate about the scope of the term, and specifically about whether it applied only to the natural world or whether human activities and human communities would have to be factored into the work of managing ecosystems. One voice said, "Stick with what you know," which meant trees and streams and animals. The other voice said, "It doesn't make any sense to manage ecosystems as if humans weren't part of them; furthermore, if we don't help timber-based communities evolve sustainable economies, they will put so much pressure on the forests that we'll never achieve sustainability there, either."

Without exactly being asked for my opinion, I found myself siding with the second voice in this debate, for reasons that had nothing to do with the mission of the Forest Service but everything to do with what it meant to be Missoula in the 1990s. As sawmills closed down throughout the region, including several in Missoula itself, I became aware of how much more resilient to these dislocations Missoula appeared than many of the smaller towns in our vicinity. In fact, Missoula seemed to be thriving as many of our smaller neighbors hung on the ropes of extinction. But for some reason I found myself increasingly nervous about that state of affairs. What had partly fueled Missoula's economy during this period was the expansion of retail and other service industries, much of the expansion coming at the expense of retail and service trade in the smaller towns. While the resulting boost in Missoula's prosperity certainly made my budgets easier to balance, I could see that we were at the same time building up a backlog of expensive social problems which were themselves a result of the decline of the economic and social fabric of the smaller towns. Sustainability could not be viewed only as an issue in the forests or the small timber-dependent communities; Missoula needed to be concerned about the sustainability of its own prosperity. The harder we looked at the issue, the more obvious it became that Missoula's long-range welfare would be better served by supporting the viability of the smaller towns around it than by growing at their expense.

Before long, the Missoula Economic Development Corporation had renamed itself the Missoula Area Economic Development Corporation, to reflect its commitment to promoting prosperity throughout the region. With MAEDC's help, the city of Missoula and the University of Montana began work on a project to map and model the economy of this region — to understand more clearly the mutually sustaining relationship between the nucleus and the rest of the cell. The Forest Service joined in, as its internal debate began to settle on the side of acknowledging that "ecosystem management" was not going to succeed without accounting for the human role in the ecosystem. What made it easier for the Forest Service to contribute to this effort was the fact, increasingly evident, that the region for which Missoula served as nucleus corresponded very closely with the Clark Fork River drainage, and therefore with a naturally bounded ecosystem.

For too much of our history, the busy-ness of cities has been perceived as a threat to the maintenance of ecological integrity. But if city-states are reemerging as primary forms of human organization at the same time that environmental awareness is assuming global dimensions, it may be because we are just now gaining an understanding that human inhabitation must become more organic if it is to conform to organic ecosystems. The adaptation of life forms to one another and to the limitations and possibilities of their surroundings is what evolution has always been about, and it is precisely such evolution and adaptation that drives the reemergence of the city-state.

In fact, what we are experiencing here in Missoula is the local equivalent of the Hong Kong story. In two entirely different settings, national governments are being brought to acknowledge that their own capacity to generate and sustain prosperity has waned, if it ever really existed, and that the organic relationship of a city to its surrounding region has to at least be enlisted as an ally if not the primary actor in that work. The magnitude of this shift can hardly be exaggerated. Nowhere in this country and almost nowhere in the world for centuries have we recognized the natural, self-defining boundaries of city-regions. The closest we come in this country is the almost entirely arbitrary lumping of several counties together for various state and federal purposes. The failure to recognize the organic, and therefore primary, character of city-regions, the tendency to treat them instead as stepchildren of the "important" political entities of state and nation, is evident in the very name we give them. Rather than letting something like Neal Peirce's "citistates" define themselves on the map, we cluster counties into "substate planning regions," as inartfully named as they are clumsily drawn.

Our political language goes far beyond this in blinding us to the natural relationships between cities and their surroundings. By referring time and again to imaginary places called, in our political discourse, "rural America," "urban America," and "suburban America," we create an image and a practice of separate urban, rural, and suburban polities, and we all but eliminate the possibility of acting upon a sound understanding of how city center, suburbs, and rural surroundings might together operate as an effective engine of economic prosperity.

A trip to Washington, D.C., near the end of my first term as mayor left me sadly wiser on this score. I was one of a dozen panelists from what the invitation called "rural America," invited to brief the secretary of agriculture on the best means of stemming the economic decline of so many rural areas. As the event unfolded, I found myself deeply impressed by the wisdom and passion of my fellow panelists from "rural America." Their consistent urging to leverage scarce federal resources by using face-to-face local collaboration to tap the immeasurable reserves of local know-how and resourcefulness seemed to me the best advice the national government could receive about how to deploy the relatively few dollars it might be able to devote to rural programs.

But it was just here that the conversation became disconcerting. I could not shake off the perception that we were in part being asked to help the Agriculture Department come up with reasons to continue to have national rural programs at all. After all, if the truly effective resources are regional or local, why strain so hard to find some "networking" or "clearinghouse" or "leadership training" role for the national government? "Because we have to do something," the very walls of the imperial auditorium seemed to whisper, "or else why would we need to be here?"

As I listened to my colleagues make their case, it occurred

to me that there might be a vastly more efficient mechanism for accomplishing all the laudable human resource–mobilizing objectives the panelists were asking the secretary and his department to pursue. Throughout history, the role of cities has been precisely to focus, organize, and multiply the resources of the surrounding regions to which they are organically connected. In the era of the nation-state, we had not only lost sight of this role, but what is worse, national policy had misled both cities and their rural surroundings into believing that they could prosper independently of one another, especially if each of them could open a wide enough pipeline to Washington. It would be difficult to overstate the extent of damage this well-intentioned national legacy has imposed upon the only sustainable economies capable of addressing the long list of woes voiced by the rural panel that morning, or those voiced by my fellow mayors, whenever they got a chance to plead for more federal dollars for "urban America."

So it was that I argued to the secretary that the best long-term favor he could do for "rural America" would be to admit that there is no such place, nor any such thing as "the rural economy," just as there is no such place as "urban America" nor such a thing as "the urban economy." But there are real places like Louisville and the region surrounding it, and real economies like that of Missoula — not the city itself of roughly sixty thousand urbanites, but the city and its two dozen or so surrounding towns whose long-term prosperity depends upon our learning how to make the region operate as the natural economy it is capable of being.

If this were true, then one of the best ways for the Agriculture Department to help its rural constituents would be to insist upon a rigorous review of the long list of national policies that have exploded the natural integrity of city-regions, deluding city centers, suburbs, and rural surroundings into ignoring their mutual dependency. The result has been a gigantic and acutely nearsighted disinvestment in both central cities and rural areas, to the short-term but unsustainable advantage of that other, ultimate nonplace, "Suburban America."

David Rusk, the former mayor of Albuquerque, refers to "four decades of misguided policies that have favored suburban development over inner cities, fragmenting urban areas by race and class."[5] The nation-state response to this situation is to begin asking how new national programs can right the balance. But no conceivable amount of federal largess to either city centers or rural areas could begin to compare in magnitude or effectiveness with the reinvestment that would naturally occur if the national government were to stop enabling the illusion of these places' independence from one another.

Rusk cites the example of Seattle, where a new regional strategy resulted in the rejection of plans for a new 4,500-home suburb twenty miles from Seattle — exactly the kind of sprawl-and-flight phenomenon that national policies have so successfully encouraged. Seattle has begun to understand that its long-term viability can only be secured by acting like a city-region or city-state, and therefore it has begun to knit together the destinies of city, suburbs, and surrounding countryside. By deciding not to build a new suburb, the city-state preserves forests and, in Rusk's words, "strengthens the plan of Mayor Norm Rice to rebuild Seattle's declining neighborhoods, since it will keep demand for housing within the city higher."[6]

Rusk argues, as does Neal Peirce, that those cities that, one way or another, have maintained or recaptured the organic relationship between central city and suburbs are, by a number of measures, more successful than those metropolitan areas that have fallen for the siren song of suburban independence. Income disparities between central cities and suburbs, for example, are far smaller in the more organic city-states. It is the

dysfunctionally isolated cities that teeter on the brink of municipal bankruptcy; Rusk found that credit ratings for more
integrated city-states averaged two full grades higher than
those for disconnected inner cities. Here we have a telling
measure of the role of city-states in the larger economy: the
global bond market is signaling in unmistakable terms the fact
that organic city-states are economically far more viable than
those cities whose suburbs have let national policy persuade
them that they are independent of their central cities. Neal
Peirce goes a step further, presenting an expanding body of
research demonstrating that those suburbs showing the most
durable economic strength are the ones ringing the most economically healthy central cities.

In the 1970s, Hartford, like so many other cities, saw its
upper and middle classes drained into its surrounding suburbs, leaving the incorporated city of Hartford with a tax base
so depleted it threatened to follow downstate Bridgeport into
bankruptcy. That prospect, however, made some suburbanites
think twice, and their thoughts boiled down to this: "If Hartford dies at its core, the insurance companies might leave, and
then what will sustain the economy of the suburbs?" Hartford's mayor, Mike Peters, a former firefighter, would have
liked to offer the suburbs a chance to help pay the cost of his
fire department, which, among other municipal services, had
made it possible for the insurance industry to cluster in Hartford, creating the type of synergy so fundamental to any thriving economy. But Peters, knowing that such economic logic
was not yet apparent on its face, took more modest steps.
When a suburban selectman complained about springtime potholes in Hartford's downtown streets, Peters asked if his
wealthy suburb could send one of its crews to help patch some
of the holes. While taken aback, the selectman listened to
Mayor Peters's argument about the suburbs' dependence upon

"a Hartford that works." The selectman encouraged Peters to make the same argument to some of the other suburbs, and within weeks, thirteen of Hartford's suburbs had sent street crews to help repair the old city's streets.

In Detroit, Mayor Dennis Archer pursued a similar course. He persuaded a number of the suburbs surrounding the badly deserted central city to send not only street and garbage crews, but ten thousand of their own citizens into the central city for a major spring cleanup. These voluntary efforts may seem like nothing but Band-Aids given the depth of the problems the inner cities of Hartford and Detroit now face, but the act of healing that occurs when a suburbanite realizes, and is willing to spend a day acting on the realization, that the well-being of the inner city is essential to the well-being of the suburbs — these acts of healing, however small they may be, will yet bear a mighty harvest as they build the fundamental structure of wholeness that is the city-state.

When William A. Johnson, Jr., moved from a career as a civil rights leader to the position of mayor of Rochester, New York, he immediately began reaching out to the suburbs. As he spoke to suburban dwellers, he became intrigued by the recurrence of a refrain in which a well-educated suburbanite would respond to Johnson's appeal to pay more attention to the central city by smiling and saying, "I never go into the city, myself." "Oh," Mayor Johnson soon taught himself to respond, in a wonderfully contrived naiveté, "then you must not ever do anything." More than a little taken aback, the cosmopolitan suburbanite would invariably ask the mayor what he meant, to which Johnson would reply, "Well, the symphony, the ballpark, the museum — they're all in the city. I guess you never go to any of these places, which is fine, I'm sure, but a bit unusual." Not wanting to be thought quite that unusual, and also reminded of an important urban fact of life, the suburbanite would usually correct course, and acknowledge to Johnson, but most especially to himself, that indeed the city was more important than he had realized. The point, of course, is not that these institutions happen to be located within the city limits, but that it is of the very essence of cities to provide such opportunities, and that those who have forgotten that cities exist for the purpose of the good life might be putting at risk their own enjoyment of life.

The expanding awareness of the interdependence of city and suburb establishes a logical plumb line that inevitably leads to the recognition that not only must central cities and their suburbs acknowledge their combined wholeness if they are to thrive and prosper, but that they in turn must understand their organic relatedness to the surrounding countryside. So, for example, Mayor Jerry Abramson has insisted that Louisville begin exploring how the long-term viability of that city might depend upon the economic health of the hundreds of small towns for which Louisville serves as the hub. So Berlin has asked the German Bundestag to formally recognize and allow the city to pursue its natural connectedness to its surrounding region, as Beijing had recognized Hong Kong's relationship with Guangzhou. So every lesson I had ever learned as mayor led me to argue to the secretary of agriculture that the best favor he could do for "rural America" would be to meet with the secretary of housing and urban development and the secretary of transportation and agree to dismantle all the national programs that had made "rural America," "urban America," and "suburban America" think they could prosper in isolation from one another.

I knew, of course, that a message so outlandish (in the root sense of the word) could not be digested in a morning's briefing. But it wasn't until the end of the session that I fully understood how deeply entrenched in the very concrete of

Washington's foundations is the resistance to such an argument. Looking back, I saw a hint of it the day before when I had told one of my own senators what I intended to say to the secretary. Senator Max Baucus's response, which I found commendably wistful, was that rural senators had no choice but to fight for rural programs just to keep the growing urban centers from getting all the money. So I should have been prepared for the secretary of agriculture's closing words: "We just want rural America to get the same treatment urban America gets — no more and no less." That, I thought, was a wish that might well come true, to the deepening dismay of both rural and urban America.

An outlander can never go to Washington without being moved once again by the palpable sense of history clinging to the place. As a farm boy who became a mayor, I am always drawn to Jefferson and his elegant memorial; I am always reminded of his distrust of cities, of his impossible dream that the frontier would allow us forever to create farmers faster than people piled up in cities. The secretary of agriculture's closing words were just another version of that forlorn Jeffersonian formula for parity between the false enemies of "rural America" and "urban America." But it was Jefferson too who warned us against getting caught in the dead doctrines of a bygone age — especially his own — and who called for a revolution every now and then to keep alive the human meaning behind his timeless invocation of "the course of human events." The nation created by Mr. Jefferson's document has so commanded our attention that we can barely conceive that "the course of human events" has finally brought us to the end of the age of the nation-state, and to the renaissance of the city-state. We will not get on with the work of our own age until that realization strikes home.

SIX

A Sisterhood of City-States

Now it is not a river valley, but the whole planet, that must be brought under human control: not an unmanageable flood of water, but even more alarming and malign explosions of energy that might disrupt the entire ecological system on which man's own life and welfare depends.

Before modern man can gain control over the forces that now threaten his very existence, he must resume possession of himself. This sets the chief mission for the city of the future: that of creating a visible regional and civic structure, designed to make man at home with his deeper self and his larger world, attached to images of human nurture and love.

— LEWIS MUMFORD, *The City in History*

D ATE CITY SITS ON THE BAY near the southern end of Hokkaido, where the tiny Salamichi River, meandering down from the volcanic mountains around Toya Lake, trickles into Uchiura Bay. Pronounced "Datay," the town's name was inherited from the Samurai chieftain whom the Meiiji regime had persuaded to colonize southern Hokkaido in the 1870s. Date, then, had been in existence for about the same length of time as Missoula, a seemingly inconsequential coincidence of the kind which, in the annals of the worldwide city-to-city movement, often becomes far more important than anyone might at first expect. But with Date and Missoula, as in all such instances, the significance of a small detail such as our respective dates of settlement would only come into focus if there proved to be a larger pattern of connectedness between the two cities. It was the existence of that pattern (or its absence) that I was watching for when my wife Jeanne and I visited Date City at the beginning of my second term as mayor.

We had come as guests of the people and government of Date City, somewhat embarrassed to have the Date International Exchange Association buying our tickets for us, but deciding from what little we knew of Japanese etiquette that it would be more embarrassing to say no to the offer than to say yes. Having humbly accepted the invitation, we set off for the Orient, making only our second foray together outside North America, the first having occurred just two months earlier when we had paid an official visit to our new sister city of Neckargemünd, Germany. So it happened that in the summer of the fiftieth anniversary of Normandy and the forty-ninth of Nagasaki, we found ourselves the guests of a small city in Germany, and then of one in Japan, both diligently seeking the friendship of an American city. Such historical reflections, and musings about their human significance, seem to spring up continually in city-to-city exchanges, lending weight to the conclusion that the sister city movement itself is a phenomenon of historical dimensions.

That perception was reenforced during my visit to Neckargemünd, when the mayor of Evian les Bains, Neckargemünd's first sister city, paid a brief visit to Neckargemünd. I asked Evian's mayor, Henri Buet, and Neckargemünd's Bürgermeister, Oskar Schuster, to tell me something about the history of their two cities' relationship. They explained that it was one of hundreds of formal connections between German

and French towns and cities that had been explicitly cultivated
since the Second World War in order to overcome, on a person-
to-person level, the hatred and mistrust that had developed
between the German and French people in a series of wars
stretching back over a century and a half. Both mayors were
convinced that the emergence of an integrated European continental system could not have occurred had not hundreds of
thousands of French and German citizens spent time in one
another's towns, spurred by the promoters of the European
community and by the sister cities movement to become ac-
quainted as human beings, not as stereotypes. The founders
of the European Economic Community, or Common Market,
had established the Council of European Municipalities, and
through it, encouraged European cities to form relationships
with compatible cities in several different European countries.
That effort led to more than five thousand formal "links" in
Europe alone, out of somewhere close to twenty thousand
city-to-city relationships worldwide. The concentration of linkages in Europe is frequently cited as a fundamental factor in
the Europeans' willingness to lay aside centuries of national
mistrust and move toward continental cooperation. Among
other things, the establishment of one-on-one links creates of
necessity an even larger number of secondary, "sister-in-law"
links of the kind Missoula now has with Evian. While we have
no direct link to Evian les Bains, the fact that Neckargemünd is
Evian's sister has created a sense of loyalty among many Missoulians to that French city, so that at the very least, we are
more likely to buy Evian than any other bottled water, and not
likely to plan a trip to the French Alps or Lake Geneva without
a stop in Evian. Within Europe itself, these secondary links,
building on a critical mass of primary connections, have played
no small part in the transforming work of the sister cities
movement.

The historically powerful side of the sister cities phenomenon only arises because of the far more subtle pattern of connectedness which gives the movement its astonishing vitality. It was in these details that Jeanne and I found ourselves taking the deepest delight on our journeys east and west that summer. Our visits to both Date and Neckargemünd had been timed by our hosts to coincide with major festivals in each of the two towns. In Neckargemünd, I donned a leather apron and assisted Bürgermeister Schuster in performing the age-old mayoral function of tapping the first keg for the Menzer Park Fest.

In Date, the apron was replaced by a short, brocaded cape, a mere shadow of the long robe and tall pointed hat Mayor Abe (pronounced "Abay") wore to open the Date Musya Matsuri, the annual harvest festival commemorating the samurai colonization of Hokkaido in 1870. The second day of the festival featured hundreds of people dressed in traditional military garb, surrounding nearly fifty fully armed and armored samurai riders (to the tune, we learned, of about $10,000 per outfit). Some riders were mounted on massive draught horses, some on Japanese thoroughbreds, and a few on a tiny breed of pony native to Hokkaido long before the samurai arrived. Each rider, each fierce set of armor, represented an old Date family, and each family's name and brief history were read aloud as its rider trotted past the standing-room-only grandstand and the reviewing platform where we sat with Mayor Abe. This painstaking communal remembrance of the history of Date families added depth to an occasion whose pageantry promised to be unforgettable in any event. This recalling of ancestors also cast a new light on what had so impressed me during the festival's opening event, the night before.

Then we had joined Mayor Abe in an upper room overlooking Date's main intersection to watch a parade. Like most parades I had seen, this one was dominated by a series of floats — floats unlike anything I had ever beheld. All these dashes ("dashays") were constructed atop small, two-wheeled trailers something like a boat trailer. The dashe rises perhaps ten feet above this conveyance, lighted from within so that in the dark streets the dashes look like huge lanterns, each rectangular side made of rice paper, each panel painted with a scene of samurai fierceness or with some mythological figure from which that fierceness had drawn its inspiration and energy.

And energy was the order of the day (or rather the night). The dashes were not drawn, as they would be in America, by a motor vehicle, but by a troop of teenage boys who would push the float down the street at a brisk trot, stop at each intersection and twirl the dashe on one spot as fast as their legs could churn until, on a whistled signal from their leader, they would rear back, straining to arrest the rotary motion they had created, and then, having brought the cart to a standstill, speed off in the opposite direction, legs and hair flying, faces glistening with sweat in the August heat.

As we watched one after another glowing dashe twirled before us in this frenzy of adolescent vitality, we learned from Mayor Abe that each dashe was sponsored by a neighborhood, a business establishment, or a club of some sort, and that the adults of the business, club, or neighborhood had overseen both the construction of the dashe and the recruitment and "training" of its drivers. They had overseen as well the recruitment and rather more exacting training of the drumming, marching, and dancing troupe that accompanied each dashe. Comprised mostly of teenage girls, often intermixed with a few women and now and then a little girl or two, these troupes all performed a highly stylized dance drawn from the traditions of the samurai era. Sometimes the dance would be performed to music drawn straight from MTV, but it always returned to a samurai leitmotif played on huge drums, which blended remarkably well with the American music now native to these youngsters' postmodern lives.

Somehow, the city of Date had managed to create an event that all generations thoroughly enjoyed, where teenagers could have the experience of knowing that their contribution was not only appreciated by the city, but was in fact central to the festival's success. During the course of the celebration, I asked dozens of questions to find out how Date had accomplished this feat, because I, like so many other American mayors, had become convinced that nothing would do our cities more long-term good than the engagement of teenagers with the life of their city. There were, of course, no simple answers to my questions; there was no recipe I could translate into English and follow, step by step, back in Missoula. But here at the festival, and in other quarters of the city, I began to see a pattern from which I thought we could learn something, and from that pattern I began also to understand that Date's leaders, both elected and citizen leaders, were intent on pursuing some ongoing connection with Missoula primarily because of their own devotion and dedication to various kinds of learning.

The first contacts between the two cities had focused on learning in its formal, institutional sense. The junior and senior high schools in the two communities had begun a series of meetings between teachers and administrators which finally led to an arrangement for a dozen or so junior high school students to come to Missoula for a few weeks during the autumn following our visit to Date, with the expectation that Missoula students would visit Date the next year. In the course of the rather complex set of discussions leading up to these exchanges, I had gradually become aware of the support and encouragement that a group of Date business leaders (all born after World War II) were putting into the effort. Some of them actually accompanied their school officials on one of their trips to Missoula, and it was these same businessmen (for they were in this case all men) who had raised the money to fly Jeanne and me to Hokkaido. Such dedication and generosity in the cause of international exchange intrigued me, and at one dinner in Date with these postwar entrepreneurs, I risked a breach of some lurking rule of etiquette by asking them what motivated their actions. All of them, I knew by now, were serious entrepreneurs, but they readily confirmed my conclusion that none of their businesses were likely to benefit directly from any contacts they might make in Missoula. Theirs was a more subtle strategy.

There were in fact at least two entrepreneurial dimensions to their activity, but it became clear that neither was intended to pay direct or immediate dividends. On the one hand, as I would hear repeatedly at other stops on my tour of Hokkaido, that northern island had become increasingly uncomfortable with the dominance of Honshu and of the highly centralized Tokyo- and Osaka-based corporatism so predominant in the economic life of Japan. Date's entrepreneurs were not alone, I would soon learn, in believing that the long-term viability of Hokkaido's economy might be better served by developing some contacts to the rest of the world that were not always brokered or controlled by "Japan, Inc."

But the restiveness with the established order that I perceived among these "Young Turks" of Hokkaido reached even beyond questions of centralization and state-sponsored corporatism. Successful as they knew their parents' generation had been in capturing vast shares of Western markets, these younger entrepreneurs now watched the yen rapidly redefining itself against foreign currencies. They knew, without being told by their elders, that unless they became very smart very fast, their familiar balance-of-trade honeymoon would soon come to a jolting halt.

Over a leisurely Korean-style barbecue (itself a reminder of another facet of Japanese history), then, I asked this generation of entrepreneurs why they were spending precious time and money on student and mayoral exchanges between Date and Missoula when they knew they would see no direct benefits to their businesses and when, if anything, they should be investing scarce resources in measures to improve their competitiveness.

Yumiko Kikuya, our hostess for our "home stay" that evening, interpreted for us, and it was her husband, Tatsuo, a prospering construction contractor, who finally brought the matter into focus for me. In effect, he told me that an entire generation of Hokkaido entrepreneurs had decided that they could only hope to succeed in the global marketplace if they could come to know other people and other cultures much more fully and comprehensively than they had done so far.

"But don't your trade magazines teach you that?" I asked Yumiko to ask him. He smiled at me, silently acknowledging that I was right in assuming that their business magazines, like ours, indeed tried their best to convey such lessons. "We need to know what people in other countries, including yours, are really like," he told me through Yumiko, holding my eyes insistently with his gaze as she translated. "There is no way to learn that except by getting to know the real life, the full life, of your people. And we can't experience that except by seeing how they live in their communities."

The intensity with which Tatsuo spoke convinced me that he had given this some thought, and that he was glad to be given a chance to speak. For my part, I certainly felt that I was getting my question answered, but not without raising several equally difficult questions. What exactly was the relationship, for example, between the profit motive and the desire for cultural enrichment? Could these business owners be so deeply cynical that they would send their children to our schools just to deepen their understanding of our consumption patterns and vulnerabilities? That question, at least, I did not have to embarrass myself by asking, although I did need it answered. But the answer was evident in the way our hosts watched and read our faces as we tested their favorite foods, all the time asking us a stream of questions about our own customs. Learning about other societies was to them its own reward, and they obviously enjoyed every minute of it and knew that in those terms alone it was worthwhile to send their children to Missoula.

When Tatsuo said that they would learn the most by seeing our people in their home settings, in their home communities, he reminded me that they were not undertaking this exchange simply as individuals, but that they were doing it as citizens of Date; they were doing it on behalf of their city, and especially on behalf of the future city of their children. Satisfying as cultural exchange might be, it could not happen to any extent unless their city's economy continued to thrive. This generation had come to believe that neither they nor, still less, their children could assure the viability of Date's economy unless they broadened their horizons substantially — unless they became, indeed, global citizens. Yet, surprisingly, they, and we in Missoula, and by now millions of other people engaged in tens of thousands of other city-to-city exchanges around the world, were finding that the surest, most satisfying path to global citizenship wound through the streets of their own city and those of one or two carefully chosen partner cities in some other quarter of the globe.

This phenomenon of city-to-city relationships has proven

tremendously powerful in the few decades of its existence, expanding at a genuinely exponential rate. When Richard Oakland moved, in 1967, from his office at the National League of Cities to the newly incorporated Sister Cities International organization, there were about 100 American cities with some kind of formal relationship with a foreign city. When Oakland retired a quarter century later, 1,000 American cities were involved in 1,600 relationships, reaching into 115 countries across the globe. Those 1,600 connections constituted roughly one-tenth of the city-to-city relationships existing worldwide, and if recent expansion continues at its steadily accelerating rate, there will be 50,000 formal linkages soon after the turn of the century.

It is all but impossible to determine when the sister cities movement began. Oakland, who has studied it as closely as anyone, jokes that "It may have started when Marc Antony set out from Rome to visit Cleopatra in Alexandria," and continues more seriously to suggest that its true roots would have to be sought as far back as the various historic ages of the city-state. In the modern era, different forms of city-to-city connection have existed for generations, many of them keyed to namesake connections, as in the link between Toledo, Ohio, and Toledo, Spain, while others grew out of preserved or unearthed links between colonies and home cities. New Bern, North Carolina, for example, has in various ways maintained contact with Bern, Switzerland, for three centuries, but their formal sister city relationship dates from after the Second World War.

In fact, it was that war and the immediately succeeding cold war that established the sister cities movement as a historical phenomenon. The nature of World War II meant, in Oakland's words, that "tens of thousands of people who had never been abroad before were flung all over the globe," where, inevitably, they came into contact with people from backgrounds very different than their own. Discovering, as Oakland says, that "these people are more like us than we thought," these repatriated warriors were eager to respond when President Eisenhower convened a White House conference in 1956 to launch what he called a "people-to-people campaign."

"Bomb shelters were the rage just at that very frigid point during the cold war," Oakland recalls, "and Eisenhower wanted to warm things up a little." The call for people-to-people exchanges (which were not intended to be confined to the Soviet Union) sounded good to many of Eisenhower's former soldiers, and with global travel more accessible than ever before, many of them could now afford to do it. But, as Oakland says, "Just going back as tourists, entirely on your own, could be intimidating, whereas if you had a home away from home to serve as a base, it seemed much more manageable."

Those cities that had responded to Eisenhower's call by establishing sister city relationships could provide their travelers with such a home base, and soon other cities, observing this advantage, followed suit. This, then, was one of the factors fueling the rapid growth in the sister cities movement. European cities, already urged to establish such relations across their own continent, began bringing their positive experiences to America, searching for opportunities here to replicate what they had found so fruitful in Europe. And by then the movement had spread far beyond the two continents bracketing the North Atlantic; it had become in every sense a global phenomenon, endowed with a powerful internal dynamism.

A phenomenon so vital does not lend itself to any simple or simply linear analysis, any more than its nearest human correlate of friendship can be reduced to some mechanical formula.

Yet it is an ancient mathematical formula that always comes to my mind when I try to understand why the emergence of global citizenship has been so strongly accompanied by the growth of the sister cities movement. When the ancient Greeks were confronted by a problem of relating something very large to something quite small, they resorted to the notion of the golden mean. Expressed mathematically, the golden mean is represented by B in the proportion: $A/B = B/C$. Thus, the golden mean between 1 and 100 is 10, since 1 stands to 10 as 10 stands to 100.

The challenge of globalism is just the kind of problem of scale to which the golden mean was meant to be applied. Most of us are simply overwhelmed by the thought of exercising global citizenship in any meaningful sense, when we realize that each of us represents less than one five-billionth of the world's population. To the extent that we attempt to practice global citizenship from that perspective, we remain restricted to excellently motivated but somehow always rather pathetic individual acts on the order of washing and reusing plastic food bags. I am reminded of the inherently comic nature of this kind of civics when, on a particularly busy morning, moved by some irresistible mood of defiance, I simply refuse to wash the day's portion of plastic bags, stuffing them instead into the garbage, and so sending them off to the landfill.

This in turn always reminds me of a stretch of several months when my youngest son, Sam, then about eight years old, refused to eat margarine or butter, taking his bread plain in order (as he wryly explained at each slice) "to save the world." He never described just what earth-saving features his abstinence comprised, and we did not ask, in part because, in his role as youngest brother, Sam had become, by observation and imitation, a kind of distillation of his older siblings' devoted practice of the art of irony. There is no point in asking what someone means when he speaks in that mode; you can only hope that meanings might reveal themselves as time goes by. In the case of Sam's butter, he had at least provided what would become a handy way for me to sum up for myself the peculiar mixture of care, commitment, and futility that seems to cling to so many individual efforts at world citizenship.

It was Sam I found myself thinking of as I watched Date's samurai dancers pass before us, troupe after troupe, and began to notice how often a group of dancers would include, among the women and teenage girls, one or two seven- or eight-year-old girls. Always my attention riveted on these girls, fascinated by their courage in taking on this fairly complex dance in public, years before they were really quite up to it. They all had to call on their full reserve of peripheral vision, straining to follow the movements of mothers, aunts, or older sisters while maintaining as steadily as possible the fixed forward gaze which was itself part of the choreography. Watching this dynamic repeated each time one of the younger girls appeared, I soon realized that many of the older girls, now so self-contained within the dance, had started here many years earlier, coming to their current ease and grace by years of practice and many a resort to these same sidelong, studying glances. It was in the center of the dance that they had learned to dance, and it seemed to me that Date was teaching itself world citizenship in much the same way.

No single one of Date's entrepreneurs, for example, had set out to learn alone the intricacies of a foreign culture, in part because on their own they would never get much deeper into the matter than their trade magazines could take them. Many of them had been tourists in America, but as tourists they would never learn what they wanted to know about American culture. By getting to know how another small city worked, though, they might. In any event, it was not simply individuals they wanted to educate; it was the future of Date itself that most strongly motivated them, and in order to influence the city's course, they needed as many of its citizens as possible to partake in this education. So the city of Date had become the student, just as the city of Missoula had become its subject of study, while Jeanne and I had been invited to their festival to whet Missoula's appetite for a little education of its own.

At the Korean barbecue, as Tatsuo explained to me why Date needed a city to learn from if its children's generation were to thrive, two of those children walked into our dining room. They and their friends were having their own party next door, but their parents wanted them to meet the mayor of the city they were about to visit. These two boys, it turned out, were to be among the junior high students visiting Missoula in the fall, and they were being coached for their adventure. As the introductions proceeded, the father of one of the boys, a golf course owner who had kept us laughing all evening with his exuberance, insisted that the boys introduce themselves in English. "Hello, my name is —" he prompted in his own self-deprecating English, and "Hello, my name is Yuhei Ookoshi," his apprentice haltingly but bravely responded. I stammered out my all-too-obviously unperfected "Hajimemashite," doing my unintentional part to reassure Yuhei that however preliminary his English might be, it was certainly better than my Japanese.

Here, as on the street watching the smallest marchers, I was reminded of the widely rediscovered adage that "It takes a village to raise a child" — but now I felt that it might also take a village, or a city like Date, to turn a child into a world citizen. Here was the golden mean at work in its classic manner, mediating between the imposingly great and the aspiringly small, creating a challenging but manageable path into the world at large. Toying with the old Greek formula, I calculated that the golden mean between an individual like Sam or Yuhei and the five billion other people inhabiting the earth would be a number just over seventy thousand — roughly the population of the Missoula Valley. If this old concept had anything to teach our era, the lesson could be that an individual's relationship to the other citizens of his or her community might come to be paralleled by the relationships among communities across the globe. Seventy thousand cities could relate to each other in the way that same magnitude of people could relate to each other within a single community.

This evocation of the golden mean should be understood in the same sense as Sam's refusal to eat butter: it should not, in other words, be taken too literally. I am not, for example, prepared to argue that the perfect size for a city is seventy thousand people. But the underlying intuition that meaningful global citizenship might be more achievable if the individual and the world were mutually served by intermediate structures of wholeness — this perception deserves careful attention. For centuries we have steadfastly denied the fundamental wisdom of the golden mean, insisting that matters of scale could be dealt with in purely abstract or mechanical terms, with no reference to the human measure of things. It was this forced denial of human scale that lay at the heart of the formation of nation-states, against the humanist pleas of the old republicans like Rousseau and Montesquieu, who insisted that democracy would fail any time people lost sight of one another. It is the recovery of this foundational appreciation of human scale that explains so much of the postnational renaissance of the city, and it is precisely the potential of the city to mediate between the individual and the earth itself that accounts for the insistent appeal of the sister cities movement.

We will not understand the historic force of this appeal if we overlook how firmly rooted it is in the organic wholeness of the cities involved. The relationship might be thought of as paralleling that of cells, organs, and animals. Cells have a definite structure and an integrity of their own. In physiological terms, they are exactly parallel to what Christopher Alexander means when he refers to "structures of wholeness" within a city. Alexander's structures, when related to one another in an organic way, create "larger structures of wholes around themselves." Perhaps the most fundamental examples of such structures within a city are neighborhoods. It is almost impossible to imagine a well-functioning city of any size that is not composed of neighborhoods with a sense of identity, a structure and a wholeness of their own. In the same way, the integrity or wholeness of cells is indispensable to their capacity to group themselves into meaningful, functioning organs. And were it not for the intervening integrity and wholeness of organs between the microorganism of the cell and the macroorganism of the animal itself, nothing resembling human life would be possible.

It is because cities are, at their best, "structures of wholeness" that they have the capacity to mediate between human beings and the emerging wholeness of the earth. Understanding how this might work requires careful attention to the intensely human dimension both of cities and of the sister cities movement.

City-to-city relationships, like human relationships, vary widely in their depth and quality. But, like human relations, the best and most satisfying city connections are those in which the cities meet and appreciate one another in a number of different dimensions. Richard Oakland, who has observed all degrees of success in these relationships, says, "The programs work best when you have many sublinks: rotary club exchanges, soccer teams, radio stations, pen pals, exchanges of newspapers." Oakland holds up the example of Portland,

Oregon, and Sapporo, the capital and metropolitan hub of Hokkaido: the two cities have established more than one hundred of what Oakland calls sublinks, and the result, he argues, is a synergy among the various connecting wires "that allows the sister city committees to take on bigger issues, such as trade relations and various forms of professional development." Sapporo and Portland, for example, have arranged live television exchanges through satellite uplinks, allowing the two cities, in effect, to talk to each other in real time. San Diego and Vladivostok conducted a similar "electronic town meeting," linking five thousand people from each city in a celebration of a new era of commerce (of every kind) between the two Pacific ports.

What makes this level of communication possible is what Oakland calls the ripple effect, which occurs when many sublinks exist between the two cities. "A child becomes a multiplier," Oakland claims, "whenever a pen pal in Sapporo writes to ask what Portland is like." The child is likely to ask his or her parents for help in describing the city; the parents in turn may recount that conversation to neighbors or colleagues, who, with so many other links already existing between the two cities, are that much more likely to have had first- or second-hand contacts of their own, which are then recounted back down the chain. As the threads of these stories circulate, they bring the sister city more clearly into focus as a human enterprise, rather than the abstraction it must have been to most people at the beginning of the relationship. Conversely, when the relationships are too thin or one-dimensional, they never achieve this synergy, and the two cities never come alive for each other.

Missoula's first sister city relationship, with Palmerston North, New Zealand, had not flourished under previous mayors, and I could not seem to do any better, apparently because the range of contacts between the two cities was simply too narrow, never expanding very far beyond the original exchange of faculty between their university and ours. When I became mayor, I found an appointment with a delegation from some city somewhere in the world on my calendar every month or two, many of them exploring the possibility of establishing a formal relationship with Missoula.

Concerned about repeating the mutually disappointing experience with Palmerston North, I took the position that I would only be willing to recommend a second sister city for Missoula if the range of potentially sustainable contacts reached into several quarters of the city's life. When a citizen of Neckargemünd, an exchange professor from the University of Heidelberg, came to see me with a message from Neckargemünd's mayor, he found my skepticism in full flower, although I was certainly eager to learn why he thought our two cities might have more in common than appeared on the surface. In this case, Erich Pohl and his Missoula counterpart, Jerry Fetz, had already done some homework, and Erich hastened to tell me that he had also brought a letter from the director of the major physical rehabilitation center in Neckargemünd to the smaller but growing regional rehabilitation center at Missoula Community Hospital. Before our two cities ever even spoke the words sister cities ("Partnerstädte") to each other, we had exchanged choirs, college students, contacts among retired citizens, and notes about common concerns over wastewater treatment and traffic congestion. Later, we sent to Neckargemünd a gift of over one hundred books by Missoula writers, and when Jeanne and I paid our official call in 1994, our delegation proudly opened an exhibit of works by Missoula artists.

A Sunday morning champagne reception in the Neckargemünd museum taught me more about the educational and humanizing effect of the sister cities movement than any of the prior events had done. During my two visits to Germany, each time with a delegation of other Missoulians, I had been surprised and slightly amused by the way the word spread across Europe that Missoula was, during this particular week, visiting Neckargemünd. University of Montana exchange students would show up out of the blue from Italy or Belgium, or a young army couple from Missoula now based in Heidelberg would drive over to Neckargemünd, or a family visiting Switzerland would suddenly change its plans to include a detour into the Neckar Valley. This, I have finally understood, is a fairly common experience — the experience of sister city as magnet, crossroads, or base camp. That morning at the museum it still seemed mysterious to me, and I was astonished by how many more Missoulians were present than the dozen or so in our official delegation.

Their numbers gave Missoula a personal presence that we could not have otherwise provided among the scores of Neckargemünd natives who had come out to see what kind of art Missoula produced. We were all eager to turn our pride in our artists to some good use by telling our hosts about the personalities of the individual artists, or about the local scenes that had inspired some of the pieces. Comparing notes with other Missoulians in the crowd, I found that many of them noticed in the course of the morning what I too had gradually recognized: that these drawings and paintings, in their mix of passion, wonder, and (perhaps above all) whimsical irreverence, expressed something about Missoula that we could never have put into words. Especially for those of us who had been away from Missoula for months or even years, the exhibit's evocation of Missoula's character was like a homecoming, and even some of us who had been gone for only a few days felt a rather ridiculous pang of nostalgia for the old home town. I understood, then, what a student from Yerevan, Armenia, had meant when he wrote, after a youth exchange in which he had had a chance to visit Yerevan's sister city of Cambridge, Massachusetts: "It helped us to realize who we were."

In the same way, our effort to convey to Neckargemünd something about the essence of Missoula had, as it turned out, focused our own understanding of our city and indeed of our selves. What had started as a "cultural exchange" in the sense of culture as frosting on the surface of life had become cultural exchange in the deeper sense of "local culture" — that which expresses as nothing else can what a place is all about.

The old phrase "genius loci" suddenly made sense to me. Missoula did have its own local genius, its own peculiar way of living out the relationship between nature and human nature. Individual Missoula artists had experienced the need to work out that relationship in a great variety of ways, and their work certainly reflected that variety; yet somehow, this collection did manage to capture and convey that which sets Missoula apart, that genius loci that identifies Missoula, that communal identity into which people must weave their individual identities as they themselves become Missoulians.

In the way Missoula sought to make itself known to people who had never seen it and in the ways we seek to know another city, like Neckargemünd or Date, the interwoven wholeness of human life, the viewing of life from every angle is simply indispensable. The art exhibit worked so well because it portrayed Missoula from enough revealing angles to convey the city's authenticity. But an art exhibit by itself is still only one way of portraying a city, and therefore only one of the ways in which cities would seek to introduce themselves to one another. Date City had invited us to attend its annual samurai festival because its citizens knew that in it, we would see many facets of their city, from the reverent recollection of their past to the preparation for their future — and in fact we saw, heard, and tasted all that and more. We could not, of course, comprehend anything close to the full identity or personality of Date even in those event-packed days, which is why these city-to-city exchanges are meant to be ongoing, growing, year-after-year phenomena.

The key to it all is that there is such a thing as the self-contained identity of your own city and the identity of another, which, although it can never be fully known in part because it can never be fully realized, still exists as that which gives a city its unique personality, and within which its citizens seek and occasionally achieve their own identity and whatever they will achieve of their own human wholeness.

It is in this complex, subtle process of achieving greater human integration and wholeness through knowing and celebrating the wholeness of human communities that the world-healing work of the city-to-city movement occurs. "It's pretty hard," Richard Oakland says, "to go to war against someone you know, and know well." A few years ago, young soldiers from Albuquerque, New Mexico, and from Ashgabat, Turkmenistan, had been trained by their respective nation-states for world-shattering conflict. In August of 1994, Albuquerque and Ashgabat, now sister cities, conducted their first reciprocal youth exchange, focusing on soccer and baseball, and on an activity more binding than any of the others: horsemanship. The New Mexican teenagers were thrilled at the chance to ride the famous Turkmen horses, while their counterparts, on their journey to Albuquerque, visited Indian pueblos and the Museum of the Horse, learning how at least three vastly different cultures shared a common awe and appreciation for this great animal.

Albuquerque and Ashgabat may by that time no longer have been a threat to each other, but city-to-city exchanges often do address immediate, deeply troubling conflicts. A youth exchange program between Omaha, Nebraska, and Braunschweig, Germany, is intended to compare notes and offer encouragement to each community's efforts to deal with the challenges of tolerance for ethnic minorities — Omaha's Latino and Braunschweig's Turkish minorities. Just knowing, not from a textbook but from real life, that another community on another continent struggles with the same kinds of problems your city does can make it easier to carry the struggle forward. While I was in Hokkaido, I visited with people in Sapporo about a special grouping of northern cities, Winter Cities International, which sponsors meetings every two years to talk about mutual problems, such as snow removal, and mutual opportunities for cultural enrichment, such as winter sports. In such settings, we are reminded that not only do individual human beings share common characteristics, common joys and sorrows across the globe, but that the work of being a city, and of striving to be a good city, is much the same everywhere, and that the differences are more apt to arise from natural conditions (such as snow and ice) than from more artificial distinctions, like those encased in national boundaries.

In these and a thousand other ways, the earth itself might be understood as employing the sister cities movement to advance its own emerging wholeness, as a way of perpetuating its organic capacity to sustain and nurture life. At a time when global warming and ozone depletion leave us little choice but to become aware of the planet as a living organism, the need for some postmodern equivalent of the golden mean, mediating between the individual and the earth, has become compelling. However, this mediation will not be effective if our attention is focused exclusively on the planet's woundedness; we must also have opportunities to celebrate its capacity to heal itself. "Mortals dwell," Heidegger wrote, "in that they save the earth [but] saving does not only snatch something from danger. To save really means to set something free into its own presence."[1] The city's ancient work of creating presence, in which humans may gladly dwell, is what now enlivens the sister cities movement, by making the living planet present to so many of its citizens. The good city — the living city — thus in its wholeness provides the context within which global citizenship becomes a genuine possibility. But that possibility can only be realized if we become steadily more aware of the living wholeness of our own cities. Before they can "save the earth," cities must understand and live into their organic relationships with their own neighborhoods, their own families, and their own immediate surroundings, relationships that form the true, mediating "structures of wholeness" between the individual and the living earth.

SEVEN

The Good Politician

In this town somewhere there sits a calm, intelligent man,
who doesn't know what he's about to do!

— RUMI, *Quatrains*

NOTHING HAS SO CEMENTED the sister city relationship between Missoula and Neckargemünd, Germany,
as these occasions on which our choirs have performed together, bringing their respective strands of training to bear on a
series of songs, reminding both the singers and all of us who
can only admire their talent what it means to share a form of
human expression developed over many centuries, carrying
within the practice certain shared skills and standards of excellence that enable these musicians, by their smiles for one another at the conclusion of a difficult piece, to say in a language
neither German nor English, "That was well done."

On the occasion of the formal dedication of our sister city
relationship, I sat beside Bürgermeister Oskar Schuster in a
Neckargemünd auditorium while our two choirs performed
Brahms' Lieder together. I heard him murmur "Sehr schön"
as he applauded their performance, and then, as we moved to
the reception following the ceremony, I watched him work the
crowd as only a politician would do. It struck me then that the
admiration and the sense of fellowship I had come to feel for

this colleague arose from sources not unlike those feeding the mutual appreciation of our musicians for one another. For several days, accompanying Mayor Schuster into every corner of his city, I had observed and delighted in the skillful work of a master politician. I had seen him chatting up the old women selling handcrafts under an awning at the Menzer Park Fest, or pulling his car over to encourage a police officer not to be too strict about parking violations in the crowded streets surrounding the festival, and had recognized in each setting the skillful interweaving of human threads that makes up the work of any politician. For a moment here at the reception, watching him navigate the shoals of German partisanship as he entertained and cajoled opposition members of the city council, I let myself think that the words "musician" and "politician" might not have to evoke such divergent responses as they ordinarily do. It occurred to me that these words might not accidentally end with the same set of letters, that in each case there can be described a specific set of skills and a rigorous standard of excellence that might lead, after a difficult passage, to a nod and a smile signifying in some universal language, "That was well done!"

I understood of course that, of all the arguments I might make to my own city council about why we should spend time, let alone money, on a sister city relationship, the argument least likely to succeed would be that I or they might learn to be better politicians. Good musicians were a comprehensible category, one that could be appreciated by most of our citizens. Good politicians sounded a little like good bank robbers: it wasn't a skill you would ask your constituents to invest tax dollars in. Caught in the thick of politics back in Missoula, I might be inclined to share that skepticism, but something about the distance and the difference of this German city put the matter, for these few days, in a new light.

Watching like an apprentice the easy, almost instinctive deployment of Mayor Schuster's political skills in the ancient halls and streets of his city, I began to think that his title itself might carry a reminder of an equally ancient human wisdom. Bürgermeister Schuster was not really the "master" of his city; he could not simply dictate events, as his tireless efforts to build support and alliances clearly revealed. But he was undeniably a master at his trade, and I was more than willing for a few days to make him my mentor. The more closely I watched, the more I came to see that, if his mastery was not *over* his city, it was still *of* his city.

As with the musicians, who learned most from each other by singing together, I would learn most from Oskar by working with him on a politically demanding project. Our one common project, of course, was the formation of the sister city, or *Partnerstadt*, relationship. Here I could watch, close up, the challenges Mayor Schuster faced; I could compare them with the challenges I confronted in Missoula, and above all I could try to incorporate into my practice the skills and techniques I saw Oskar deploy. Here, because we were trying to create something together, we could also practice our politics together, and in that context improve our skills. I knew without asking that Oskar was counting on me to use whatever political skills I might possess to help him consolidate among his council members and leading citizens the support that would be required to make the *Partnerstadt* work in Neckargemünd. I understood what he wanted because I had counted on him in just the same way in Missoula.

I knew, for example, that Oskar hoped I could help the four Green Party members on his city council see facets of value in the relationship which they might never recognize or at least never quite trust when presented from his conservative Christian Democratic Union point of view. I could speak confidently of Missoula as a relatively green city, a city intent on solving many of the same kinds of environmental problems the Greens were committed to addressing in Neckargemünd. I was, as it happened, personally in a position to establish credibility with them because, as one Missoulian observing the scene put it, "They can see that green stripe on your own forehead." After observing Oskar's well-seasoned political style as well as his ideological leanings, I concluded that I was probably greener than he in more ways than one, but his political acumen made him more than willing to have me display my environmental credentials, since it would help him build the support he needed, on his delicately balanced council, for this sister cities project which meant so much to him.

If this description of Mayor Schuster's mode of operation (or even the description of his working the crowd at the reception) makes him sound cynical and manipulative, I want to hasten to correct the picture, and yet to keep it within the realm of real politics, which I admire Oskar for practicing so well and which I am convinced is indispensable to the realization of any city's potential. And this brings us to the crux of the matter.

Across the globe, politics lies in such deep disrepute that almost anyone who holds or aspires to a hopeful view of humanity's future will either attempt to ignore politics in describing the unfolding of that future, or will put the burden of its unfolding on some other, nonpolitical (and therefore, I believe, mythical) way of ordering human affairs. The entire purpose of this book is to suggest that the refocusing of human energy around the organic wholeness of cities or city-states promises a profound rehumanizing of the shape and condition of our lives. By attending to the health of the body politic, for example, we are reminding ourselves of the ancient wisdom that individuals cannot be fully healthy, physically and mentally, in isolation, but only as meaningful players in a meaningful community. Or again, the attention to the potential of our cities is reminding us that children cannot realize their own full potential except in the context of a well-functioning community. In these and countless other ways, the healing (the making more whole) of cities is serving to heal — to reknit — the often frayed and sometimes severed strands of our humanity.

The potential lying at the heart of the living city will not be realized in spite of politics, or by replacing politics with some nonpolitical alternative. Just as the city itself, just as the city-state or polis has kept alive within its fundamental nature an essential element of humanism that is now reasserting itself in a thousand different forms, so too politics, whose very name derives from the word polis, has carried within itself that same fundamental humanism so indomitable in the form of the city. In fact, the two are inextricable, which means, first, that no city's potential can be realized apart from politics, and second, that the realization of the city's potential is, as it has always been, the real definition of politics.

But if what we seek is the human and humanizing potential in politics, we may find it more quickly if, instead of setting out to remake politics, we first make ourselves stand without blinking before that which we find unlovely or dehumanizing in political affairs. What is it, then, that makes politics so hard to love or indeed to endure? Is it just that the wrong people are drawn into politics? Or is politics the kind of activity that inevitably leads even good people astray? Lord Acton's aphorism seems to capture our fear and to express the prevailing cynicism. If "all power corrupts, and absolute power corrupts absolutely," and if politics is fundamentally concerned with power, then politics cannot help having a harmful influence on those drawn into its sphere.

My observation of cities and city leaders has persuaded me that there are hopeful signs all around us of the emergence of a more humanly sustaining and fulfilling politics. But I take issue with the views of some of my colleagues who want to believe that this more hopeful politics is preferable because it has less (or perhaps nothing at all) to do with power. I am convinced that all politics is about power, but that there are different ways of relating to power, and that it is in those differences that we have to seek sustainable signs of the humanizing of politics.

What is corrupting about power is the natural tendency for its practitioners to treat it as a personal possession, to become too attached to the personal satisfactions it affords, and to let those satisfactions determine the ways, the means, and the ends to which power is deployed. Perhaps nothing so cogently distinguishes constitutional government from despotism as the understanding, implicit in the first but absent in the second, that whatever power the politician wields, and whatever additional power he or she gains by risking the present store wisely and well, all such political power is held, risked, and expanded not in the politician's own name but only as a form of stewardship on behalf of those whose power it really is.

The great challenge of constitutional government has been to devise forms, formulas, and procedures that, while allowing and even encouraging politicians to engage in their craft, would still maintain some semblance of that stewardship. But as a growing chorus of people have argued in the past few years, the undeniable benefits of checks and balances and constitutional safeguards have carried their own dehumanizing price. "Governments of law, not of men" have tended to become, over time, mere mechanisms, a disembodied kind of politics that, even if it did succeed in containing the corrupting effect of power, would still not feel humanly satisfying precisely because we have done everything possible to remove the human element from it, in order to guard ourselves against the all-too-human weakness for the lure of power. This is what Harvard political scientist Michael Sandel means by his phrase "the procedural republic and the unencumbered self."[1] Our efforts to contain and sanitize the exercise of political power have all too often had the effect of disencumbering individuals, both citizens and politicians, from exercising the personal responsibility of working out solutions together, which alone can make democracy work.

But the resurgence of cities as potentially far more human enterprises than the politics we know and loathe brings with it a crucial reminder of a very different and even more ancient way of containing the urge to power. If our modern, highly procedural and mechanistic approach to public life has left our governments abstract and disembodied, it should remind us that the phrase "the body politic" came into being from a very different experience, an experience of feeling as if politics really could be embodied. And being embodied (as politics is in the good city) is a different, nonprocedural, and in the end far more humanly satisfying way of being contained.

If we were to remove for a moment the blinders of our cynicism, we could see, in politicians like Oskar Schuster and countless other mayors and city leaders around the world, a new blending of the age-old art of politics with the equally ancient containment offered by the embodiment of the city into the body politic. If, not altogether trusting this evidence, we were to look beyond the experience of these contemporary politicians for some historical precedent to the more humanistic politics now emerging in cities around the world, we could find two especially instructive examples in the Renaissance city-state of Florence.

The first is Nicolo Machiavelli, a choice that must immediately appear misplaced, since it is exactly the Machiavellian side of politics that many people find so deeply distasteful, and indeed so inhuman that they try to have nothing to do with politics, and would choose, if they could, to operate the world on some other principle altogether. The plotting, the horse-trading, the maneuvering and manipulation that the very name Machiavelli brings to most people's minds is precisely what they hate most about politics. It is just this image of politics that will have led most readers to smile or scoff at this chapter's title. But it is not Machiavelli the abstract thinker who can help us understand the challenges and possibilities of our own politics, but Machiavelli the Florentine. Florence, that intensely alive city, surrounds and pervades all of Machiavelli's writing, and it is this which assures us that whatever we may learn from Machiavelli about "the good politician" draws its truth and its human significance directly from the good city.

Of all his brilliant and enduring observations about politics and politicians, nothing will repay scrutiny today like Machiavelli's teaching about the role of what he calls Fortuna in the politician's life. No one has ever understood better than Machiavelli how important it is for a politician to accept the periodic intervention of fate or fortune in human affairs. The picture that emerges from a careful reading of *The Prince* is that of a politician who moves readily and gracefully from an acceptance of what is given and unchangeable in the course of events to decisive action at those moments when Fortuna does allow for genuinely effective human intervention.

It is just these subtle shifts between times ruled by what is given and times when action becomes possible that most decisively challenge the skill and instinct of the politician. "But a man is not often found sufficiently circumspect to know how to accommodate himself to the change," Machiavelli writes, "both because he cannot deviate from what nature inclines him to, and also because, having always prospered by acting in one way, he cannot be persuaded that it is well to leave it; and

therefore, the cautious man, when it is time to turn adventur-
ous, does not know how to do it, hence he is ruined."[2] The
prince, the good politician, is the one who has developed the
light-footedness to adapt to the shifts in fortune. Yet no
amount of skill can assure success in this regard, because the
risks of politics are real risks.

As a result of Fortuna's intervention, there is, Machiavelli
insists, no such thing as a guarantee that things political, no
matter how well planned, will go well. "Never let any Government imagine that it can choose perfectly safe courses," he
warns, "rather let it expect to have to take very doubtful ones,
because it is found in ordinary affairs that one never seeks to
avoid one trouble without running into another."[3] It is just his
insistence upon the inevitability of risk in the politician's work
which makes Machiavelli's political theory so fundamentally
humanist. It is of the essence of the human condition that
things can go wrong, and in the background of Machiavelli's
argument that there is no certain guarantee against such twists
of fate, we should hear a warning against our own efforts to
make politics safe by making it mechanical. But we should at
the same time catch a glimpse of Florence, the city-state, the
body politic, which in its own emerging wholeness gives scope
to the Machiavellian politician's enterprise while containing
and shaping in a strikingly nonmechanical way the results of
that risk-taking entrepreneurship.

It seems to be some appreciation for that kind of embodied
political self-containment that draws me, whenever I visit
Washington, D.C., to stand again before Verrocchio's bust of
Lorenzo de Medici, at the heart of the National Gallery's Renaissance collection. Eyes better trained than mine for appreciating fine sculpture might well be drawn to admire Verrocchio's artistic skill without ever a contaminating thought of
politics, while a patron of the arts might come simply to pay

homage to Lorenzo, arguably the greatest of all art patrons, who on that score alone deserves a memorial as endlessly engaging as Verrocchio's sculpture. But, neither art critic nor art patron myself, I am still drawn to Lorenzo the Magnificent, Lorenzo the Master Politician.

Verrocchio chose to portray Lorenzo gazing downward and slightly aside, leaving no doubt that his gaze is actually inward — so deep within, in fact, that we cannot escape the conclusion that Lorenzo's character is itself tremendously rich. I can never stand in that gallery room without feeling invited to imagine what room or corner of his own mind Lorenzo might be visiting. But this intensely provocative self-containment is balanced by an equally explicit outwardness, captured most compellingly in the elegantly expressive cap Lorenzo wears. Not everyone could wear such a cap; indeed it takes all Lorenzo's noble breeding, all the depth and centeredness we see in that inward gaze, to fit the cap so heroically to the person. Somewhere in the forever mobile balance between the inwardness and outwardness of the sculpture, the "magnificence" of Lorenzo stands forth, bringing me repeatedly back to that spot on the gallery floor.

Lorenzo's cap, and with it all the outwardness of the sculpture, evoke late-fifteenth-century Florence as the piece's true context and background. The cap is essentially a way of addressing and participating in the life of the city. And those words, "the life of the city," applied to a place as intentional about the good life as Medicean Florence, remind us again that the very word "politics" had once meant precisely "the life of the city." Lorenzo's Florence, like Renaissance Venice or Milan, was not simply a city, but a polis. The Italian Renaissance corresponds with the second great age of the city-state, and at the core of the Renaissance itself lay the rediscovery of the humanly sustaining truth, beauty, and goodness of the first age of the city-state. We tend to identify that rebirth most strongly with art, but a little reflection reminds us that Machiavelli was as much a part of the Florentine Renaissance as were his neighbors Leonardo da Vinci or Michelangelo, and that Lorenzo's politics were fully as crucial to Florence's golden age as was his patronage of the arts. Lorenzo, in the breadth and reach of his talents, was exactly what we now mean by a "Renaissance man," but to no small extent that is to say that he was thoroughly a man of his city. His breadth is a reflection, a drawing together, of the rich life of that great city. From that perspective, Lorenzo could not help being a politician, because the closer Florence drew to the classic form of the polis, the more clearly it remembered that, as a human enterprise, politics had always been precisely "the life of the polis," the life of the city.

This, then, is the beginning of the politician's encounter with the bust of Lorenzo — an acknowledgment that Lorenzo's presence, his commanding humanness, is unknowable apart from his full-bodied participation in the life of his city. In that presence, it is possible to imagine that politics might one more time, perhaps in another rebirth of the city-state, be reborn as the humanly satisfying life of the city itself. But this possibility will not be realized by denying the seemingly less exalted but no less necessary side of politics that Machiavelli so insistently represents. The politician's unique skill at engaging the thrusts of fortune is not something apart from, but something integral to, politics as the life of the city. And this, too, is present in Verrocchio's sculpture.

Famous as a man of action, Lorenzo was also known for his superb sense of timing, and it is not difficult to read in his inward gaze, with Florence so palpably present around him, some effort on his part to determine, in Machiavellian terms, where his own intervention might become a genuine possibility. Yet for all his skill at making such choices, Lorenzo stands as a potent reminder of Machiavelli's teaching that the risks of politics are real risks, not all of which will turn out well. One of the remarkable features of Verrocchio's sculpture is that it refuses to gloss over Lorenzo's obviously broken nose; in fact, nothing so humanizes the sculpture as this ill-fated result of Lorenzo's risk-taking. But even here, Lorenzo as politician stands forth as the embodiment of his city, for his risk-taking on behalf of his city is simply the leading edge of the fundamental risk-taking entrepreneurship of the city in pursuit of its self-realization. To grasp how the emerging wholeness of the city might provide a humanizing context for politics, we have to understand how fundamental such entrepreneurship is both to the city and to politics.

The longer I have practiced and observed politics, the more I have come to see it as a kind of entrepreneurship of power. Power is the capital in which politicians deal. Like any entrepreneurs, their job is to watch for opportunities to increase their capital, and like other entrepreneurs, those opportunities are almost always accompanied by risk. If the risk pays off, the capital that was invested comes back, often in a new form, slightly or greatly increased, to be risked again in some new venture. This constant round of risking, reaping, and reinvesting power is a fundamental dimension of the art of politics.

Take the common case of a city council member who decides to run for mayor. If the terms of the two offices overlap, this can be done without risking the office already held, but more often one office, where a politician might be quite secure, must be risked for an office of greater power. Assume that this council member lives in a city like Missoula, with the council elected from wards and with a "strong mayor," as opposed to a council-manager form of government. If the council member becomes mayor, then, she will be the chief executive officer of the city, undeniably a position of greater power than the one she now holds. But to get there she must put at risk the not inconsiderable power of her council seat. If she loses, she might of course run at some future time for her old council seat, but in preparing herself to run for mayor she may well have risked some of her natural support within her own ward. A credible candidate for mayor must, for example, have demonstrated a capacity to tend the interests of the entire city, not just one of its neighborhoods, and in building that credibility (itself a form of political capital), the council member may have had to disappoint some of the more parochial interests of the neighborhood that first elected her. The risking of a current store of power in an enterprise (such as running for mayor) that may increase that supply is an indispensable element of the art of politics. The subtleties of such entrepreneurship could be described in great detail, and as one who admits to loving politics, I would not soon tire of recounting the details. The point here, however, is not to describe the entrepreneurship of power for its own sake, but rather to understand what such politics has to do with the good city.

Jane Jacobs has perhaps done more than any other single writer to help us fathom how crucial a role entrepreneurship plays in the story of a good city. The endless envisioning and risk-taking pursuits for particular urban sites are the engine of change that keeps the city alive. Jacobs argues with hard-edged persuasiveness that these opportunities do not emerge out of thin air, but are always shaped by the urban context of the site itself. So the ever changing face of the city evolves through a dialectic between the character of the existing city, on the one hand, and the risk-taking imagination of a vast assortment of entrepreneurs on the other.

The range of entrepreneurship is of utmost importance to the city's vitality, and recalls our attention to something never far from the core of Jacobs's teaching, namely the living nature of the city and its ecosystem-like dependence on diversity to maintain its vitality. A good city, in other words, depends not only on imaginative people taking risks in pursuit of opportunities they see in particular locations, but also on those risk-takers being widely diverse in their dreams and their manner of pursuing them.

Given the clarity of Jacobs's perception of the role of entrepreneurship, it is surprising to note how steadfast she has been in excluding one key set of city actors from the entrepreneurial mix. Throughout her writings about cities, Jacobs portrays politics and politicians almost without exception as obstacles to the most fruitful evolution of the city, acknowledging none of the life-giving entrepreneurship she describes so vividly in other city activities. In a later book, *Systems of Survival*, turning her attention at last away from cities, Jacobs reveals why she has never seen politics as part of the city's entrepreneurial life force. The book focuses on an analysis of two contrasting moral systems: commerce and what she calls guardianship — politics and military arts. One of the key elements of her "commercial moral syndrome" is the injunction to "use initiative and enterprise," but she explicitly excludes such entrepreneurship from her "guardian syndrome," and thus from politics itself.

On this score, I think Machiavelli is right and Jacobs wrong, but if that is so, it is because Machiavelli had the advantage of the living city-state outside his study window. If Jacobs has overlooked a central (and crucially humanizing) feature of politics, the oversight is the result of our having, since the last great age of the city-state, severed our understanding of politics so radically from its roots in the city that we can no longer think very clearly about either politics or cities. But if there is to be a widespread renaissance of the good city, it can only proceed hand in hand with a recovery of politics' roots in the polis, which will in turn reveal how crucial political entrepreneurship is to the life of the city.

As a matter of fact, nothing is so prevalent in the current literature of political reform as the language of entrepreneurship. Whether it comes in the form of direct advice to political officials to encourage entrepreneurship within their organizations (as in Ted Gaebler and David Osborne's *Reinventing Government*) or in the more generalized but now thoroughly established celebration of "public-private partnerships," the prevailing wisdom teaches politicians that the path to success is to form alliances with and adopt much of the ethos of the private entrepreneur. However, if the convergence of public and private entrepreneurship is urged and pursued at all levels of government, its fruits are vastly more evident in the city than in any other arena. This is so for one simple but potent reason: while counties, states, and nations are abstractions from economic activity, cities are the embodiment of economies. Therefore, as Jacobs teaches so persuasively in her earlier books, entrepreneurship, which is at best tangential to a county or a state, is precisely what gives a city its life and its shape.

Jacobs, by denying politics its entrepreneurial role, also denies the city-state the chief means of its own regeneration, just as surely as do those writers who treat political entrepreneurship as a placeless abstraction, in the process overlooking the key role of cities in what used to be helpfully called "political economy." This phrase captured the intuition that both politics and economics are worthy of our attention precisely because of their combined humanistic potential. It is not in political or economic theory, however, but in the ordinary, day-to-day practice of city politics that we will find the material for a dynamic harmony between the ceaseless entrepreneurship of the living city and that of the true politician.

When I first met Mayor Joseph Riley at the Mayor's Institute on City Design (which he had been instrumental in founding), I was just beginning my tenure as mayor, while Riley had been mayor of Charleston for nearly fifteen years. Later, near the end of my first term, asked to serve as a juror for the American Institute of Architects' Jefferson Awards, I would have an opportunity to vote for one more in a lengthening list of prestigious recognitions of Riley's work in preserving the best of Charleston's historical features while steadily adding to the city's economic vitality and the livability and affordability of its housing stock.

Few contemporary mayors have more persistently or more successfully devoted themselves to Christopher Alexander's injunction to approach "every increment of construction . . . in such a way as to heal the city," and no mayor has earned more gratitude from architects, planners, and designers for that work. Joe Riley, however, for all his design sensitivity, is not an architect, but an artist of another sort: he is a master politician, an entrepreneur of power. And it is his skill as a political entrepreneur that has enabled him so successfully to assist Charleston in its ongoing pursuit of its own wholeness. An example of this may be found in the story of Charleston Place, a story that began shortly after Riley first became mayor in 1975.

Between King and Market streets, several blocks stood vacant or dilapidated in the heart of Charleston's historic downtown. Before Riley's election, developers had been laying tentative plans for a new hotel and convention center on the site, and opposition to the plans had also begun to crystallize. The core of the opposition were the advocates of historic preservation, people concerned about the project's plans to raze the few remaining historic buildings on the site. They were also concerned about the aesthetic fit between a large, ultramodern edifice and the surrounding historic district.

So far, the description could fit almost any city in the country, and few cities would be at a loss to come up with similar stories about standoffs between development and preservation. But this was not just any city; this was Charleston, Historic Charleston, the very cradle of the American historic preservation movement. And it was in those terms that the opposition to Charleston Place mounted its attack, calling upon preservation advocates nationwide to enter the fray. Before the episode had concluded, the matter had passed before a federal judge and a presidential panel on historic preservation. But it was at city hall, and above all in the mayor's office, that the politics of preservation and of downtown renewal slowly fashioned a solution of which almost all segments of Charleston society now feel proudly satisfied. That solution involved no small amount of mayoral jawboning on issues of facade design, building height, and so on. It also depended upon Riley persuading preservationists that a thriving downtown would do a better job of preserving its historical features than would a decaying urban core. But it is not persuasive skill alone that can account for a politician's contribution to a project like Charleston Place. Just as the developers risked their financial capital on the project, Riley risked substantial sums of his political capital.

If the project had been built and then failed financially, he would have lost an important part of his political base, and that would have been even more true if the new buildings had become a national rallying point exemplifying how development can ruin historic districts. As it turns out, Charleston Place has brought untold thousands of convention-goers to downtown Charleston, adding to the city's vitality while also spreading the reputation of Charleston as a place that has genuinely and effectively cared for its history. "Now," Joe

Riley says, "you never meet anyone who was against Charleston Place," meaning that most of those who had opposed it have long since seen its value both to Charleston's economy and to its culture. Riley does not say this in a self-serving way; he recognizes that the success of Charleston Place cannot be measured solely in terms of its healing of a wounded downtown site, but in terms of how it has helped a number of people move beyond their single-interest advocacies to a broader appreciation of what constitutes the public good. The healing of both the city's physical body and its civic self occurred in part because a skillful politician had risked his political capital (which he understood was in fact the city's own capital) on a venture that his instincts told him could work to the city's long-term benefit, but which his years of political experience had also warned him could fail.

Without such politics, no city ever has or ever will succeed in moving, as Charleston has, step by often faltering step, toward its renewal. All too seldom do we acknowledge the crucial role of the human art of politics in such renewal. But our mistrust of politics can become, and *has* disastrously become, a barrier to our democratic capacity to shape the conditions of our own existence.

One reason I felt motivated (if not obligated) to do whatever I could to help Mayor Schuster consolidate support for the sister city relationship among Neckargemünd council members was that I knew he had risked a substantial amount of his own political capital on this project. My experience in Missoula had persuaded me that any amount of public investment in global matters was like investment in public art: you could bank on a chorus of "Why are you spending money on this when we can't even find the resources to . . ." (to be filled in by the complainant's favorite unmet need, whether of the social, environmental, or pothole-filling variety). If enough people share that sentiment, it becomes a threat to the tenure of the politician who has risked his or her capital on such a project. The tendency of people to challenge and complain about such undertakings is heightened by the steadily deepening distrust of politics and politicians, which now automatically defaults to the assumption that whatever a politician decides to undertake is at best misguided, and at worst self-serving. According to this prevalent cynicism, if Bürgermeister Schuster was so intent on creating a sister city relationship with Missoula, it was probably because he was personally going to get something out of it. This negativism about the entrepreneurship of power is certainly founded in a sober and often sound assessment of human nature. But a narrow fixation on the dark side of politics can easily blind us to its healing human potential.

As we walked through the thousand-year-old streets of Neckargemünd, Mayor Schuster pointed out to me the improvements the city had made or was working on, as well as the problem areas for which no solution had yet been found. He had, for example, supported a two-hundred-apartment retirement center near a brook named Elsen, just above its confluence with the Neckar River. We were standing together on the balcony of a Green Party council member's home when Mayor Schuster pointed the site out to me, and our host took the opportunity to put forward his Green perspective that a park would have been a more suitable use for this particular piece of land. Relieved that for once I did not have to take any responsibility for the outcome of a debate that sounded all too familiar, I let my eyes wander across the intricate cityscape below me, thinking of the political choice Neckargemünd faced at this site against the background of Christopher Alexander's previously quoted description of the organic nature of cities:

When we look at the most beautiful towns and cities of the past, we are always impressed by a feeling that they are somehow organic. . . . Each of these towns grew as a whole, under its own laws of wholeness . . . and we can feel this wholeness, not only at the largest scale, but in every detail: in the restaurants, in the sidewalks, in the houses, shops, markets, roads, parks, gardens and walls. Even in the balconies and ornaments.[4]

All this lay before me as I stood on Herr Schmitz-Günther's balcony, where I could indeed "feel this wholeness," but where I was also reminded that it had not happened by accident, nor by magic, nor alone by good design, but in many cases by political decisions as difficult as the one Mayor Schuster and Councilman Schmitz-Günther were now discussing.

As I listened to their debate, as I pictured behind it the careful, skillful, chessboard maneuvering of social forces that politicians always instinctively undertake in the working out of such issues, I realized that what they were doing was certainly politics, with all its usual Machiavellian connotations, but that their political work also carried hints of the old Greek dimension of "politics" as the life of the polis. The Greeks who first used the word "politics" were themselves intensely aware of the organic nature of the polis, which meant that no small part of what they called politics was just what Alexander refers to as the evolving wholeness of the city.

As my colleagues brought the very specific skills of their trade to bear on this site-specific issue, I in the luxury of my away-from-home detachment could imagine the city below me using their skill, their intricate political dance, to carry on the never completed work of evolving its own wholeness. The city's relationship to its landscape, and simultaneously to its aging citizens, would be worked out in part on this site; what came of the solution would form part of the evolving fabric of the city. And the city had no other means than politics to work through the question of what, for the next several decades, it would make of this part of itself.

If Mayor Schuster was a master artisan, as my observations of his skill in such situations had led me to believe, then his art was in some sense the art of city-craft, of helping the city to realize its own form. In this sense, "Bürgermeister" and "politician" might be seen as the same title, both implying mastery of the art of city-craft, Bürger-craft, polis-craft. With that awareness arose a memory of a walk I had taken with Mayor Schuster in Missoula the summer before where, as I could see now, I had been trying, with his help, to understand a little more clearly my own profession and my own evolving practice of it.

When out-of-town friends visit me in Missoula, I often find myself wanting to give them some idea of what my work is about and why I find it so satisfying. I could do that just by asking them to follow me through "a day in the life of a mayor," and sometimes I have done that, but more often I ask them to spend a couple of hours walking the city with me. This walk, I realize now, has become my favorite metaphor for the work I do, which means it has become one of my metaphors for politics. Having already come to admire Mayor Schuster's political skill, and needing anyway to show him his new sister city from as many angles as possible, I invited him to accompany me on my "this is my work" walk.

We set out, then, from city hall, traversing four or five blocks of downtown Missoula, to the trail along the north bank of the Clark Fork River. The trail and the river would occupy most of our attention, but my political narrative began here on the downtown streets, and it reached back to a point well before I had become active in city politics. No one would ever have walked along the river bank in those days, in part because there was no place to walk, but also because the river had for decades been treated as Missoula's back alley where, quite literally, we had dumped our garbage.

Then, during the 1980s, Missoula began to bring its downtown business district back from a mall-induced, nearly fatal catatonia to a remarkable robustness, the heart of which was the city's rediscovery of the Clark Fork River. The mechanism for renewal had been tax increment financing. This tool is always open to the criticism that the common treasury is being used for the benefit of one specific area of urban renewal. But Missoula's leaders were wise enough to insist on the value of reclaiming the city's center. As a state legislator, my role at the outset was simply to help pass tax increment legislation, but later, as mayor, I came to appreciate the wisdom and the entrepreneurship of my predecessors. The capital they had risked had begun a healing, not only of the physical heart of the city, but of the political culture as well.

Tax increment funds leveraged private investments in facade improvements and store renovations, and as businesses began returning to the downtown, the public Missoula Redevelopment Agency (MRA) and the private Missoula Downtown Association (MDA) fashioned a solid working partnership. The city-merchant alliance spawned a contagion of storefront renewals, replete with tasteful and inviting awnings; the MRA planted street trees; and the MDA commissioned a local artist to produce scores of hanging wrought-iron flower baskets. This was precisely the work of healing the city, and it soon became apparent that the work was sustaining and extending itself. As people met under the flower baskets, they began congratulating themselves on their collective good taste. Encouraged by what they had accomplished, they extended their efforts to the long-abused riverfront on the southern edge of the old downtown. Together, the Redevelopment Agency and the Downtown Association brought the river back into focus as the city's center. We are still expanding the series of new riverfront parks, but the centerpiece will remain Caras Park, just off the Higgins Avenue Bridge. Caras Park is Missoula's one hundred percent location, not only because of where it is but because of what has been built there.

Several years ago, the University of Montana Drama Department and the Downtown Association erected a vast tent as a site for summer theater. Then, following the recommendations from a riverfront design competition, the MRA began work on a landscaped park, with a bricked piazza that could serve as a tent pad, next to a circular events ring. Once the park was completed, the MDA began hosting an event they called Out to Lunch at Caras Park. Every Wednesday at noon throughout the summer, they hired musicians to perform in the amphitheater, or in the tent next door on the rare occasion of rain.

The first summer, a few faithful officers of the MDA brought their sack lunches and huddled on the bottom steps of the amphitheater; the next summer, they brought their friends; then some food vendors showed up for the event; then more people came to see what all these other folks were doing down in the park. Now, every Wednesday, thousands of people spill onto the hillsides surrounding the amphitheater; the tent is filled with vendors, the piazza is encircled by them, and most of us would rather forget our own birthdays than miss a Wednesday noon at Caras Park. The success of Out to Lunch has led to the further development of the park, most notably the construction of an elegant building near the tent to house Missoula's new, vastly popular hand-carved carousel.

If the visitor with whom I am walking happened to be in

town on a Wednesday in summer, I would plan our walk to include a long stop at Out to Lunch. More often, though, as in Mayor Schuster's case, I will have to be content to stop by the mostly empty amphitheater, trying to describe Out to Lunch well enough that a picture of its role in the city's evolving wholeness will shape itself in his mind. After a few minutes at Caras Park, then, we begin strolling again down the river, toward the Orange Street Bridge and the political problem I want him to help me puzzle out.

Between the Higgins Avenue and Orange Street bridges, all along the edge of Caras Park, the Missoula Redevelopment Agency has built a trail on the riverbank. After years of piecing together new sections of trail like this one, many of which run through the new parks the city created along the river, the agency has developed a nearly continuous trail on the northern bank of the river from the Van Buren Street footbridge a mile upstream to the Orange Street bridge, now just ahead of us. The gradual piecing together of trail segments is what I always picture when I read Christopher Alexander's suggestion that "every new act of construction . . . must create a continuous structure of wholes around itself." The riverfront trail literally reaches out to join itself, putting pressure on the intervening parcels that prevent it from doing so, and then whenever it succeeds in filling in one of those gaps, it encourages whatever touches it to a greater wholeness as well.

Across the river, the trail between the two bridges is now in fact continuous, and it is to that southern section of the trail that I want to take my visitor. But the relaxed pleasure of our stroll must now be interrupted. There is no good way up from the trail to the Orange Street Bridge; instead, we will scramble up a steep, gravelly bank, and then at the other end of the bridge slide down an even steeper grade to the trail on the southern shore. Here, in other words, the structure of whole-ness remains incomplete, and here, in the most fundamental sense, the work of politics begins.

When I first took office and began this series of walks, the plunge to the south bank of the river dropped us into a waste-land — a stretch of riverfront mounded with gravel heaps and fill dirt in the summertime, or in winter with dump truck–sized loads of snow removed from the downtown streets. But now, where those unsightly mounds had lain so long, I meander with my guest along the winding paths laid out through our newest park — an unusual park, but one of which the mayor is clearly inordinately proud. Not smoothly manicured like Caras Park, the Clark Fork Natural Park blooms in early sum-mer with waist-high clover amid a rather motley variety of native grasses. The demure honey locusts of the north shore parks have found no home here, but a variety of young native trees and shrubs invite the imagination of what this place will come to look like as they mature. Some of the trees have invited more than imagination; several young ponderosa pines are now no more than slender stumps, their pointed tops bearing the lasting, entrepreneurial marks of beaver teeth, and bearing as well testimony to the park's obvious success in maintaining a bit of urban wildlife habitat.

From the new river viewing platform here in the Clark Fork Natural Park, we can look back across the river toward Caras Park and the trail we just walked. The two parks are so close that a visitor to one feels drawn to the other, and it is easy for us to envision people standing here, looking across to the carousel, wishing to visit that side of the river.

After our scramble up and down the steep banks of the Orange Street Bridge, we now know how much easier that crossing is to imagine than to accomplish. Mayor Schuster and I agree that what is needed nearby to link the trails is a footbridge — but here, with one breath, I have uttered one of the most politically explosive words in Missoula, a word that has been the subject of uncounted meetings, studies, hearings, and headaches. Part of my intention in taking this walk is to call on Mayor Schuster's political savvy to help me understand how to deal effectively with this knotty little issue.

Before I became mayor, the Downtown Association and the board and staff of the Redevelopment Agency had already concluded that the city should build a pedestrian and bicycle bridge linking the north and south shore trails, creating, once the gaps in the trail were closed, a continuous loop between this new bridge and the Van Buren Street footbridge. As a member of the city council, representing the neighborhoods on the south shore, I too thought this was a good idea, but I soon learned that many of my constituents did not.

The charming (and quiet) neighborhood above the south bank of this stretch of the river was not interested in the idea of a busy new park down below, with people coming to it in cars that would probably be parked on their streets, and even more people then coming from across the river by way of this proposed new bridge. When the Redevelopment Agency first proposed spending a million of its dearly saved dollars on the bridge and park, the city council withheld its approval. The council hesitated in part due to concern about whether the park should be traditional, manicured, and people-intensive, or one that preserved more of the wildness of that south shore of the river. The main cause of the council's reluctance, though, was the bridge; it had simply created too much controversy, not only from the south shore neighborhood, but from those who thought the river was becoming too cluttered, and from those who thought that if the downtown merchants wanted it, it must be suspect on some grounds. In effect, then, the city council suggested to the MRA board that it continue to consider the possibility of a park, but with no bridge providing access to it from the downtown.

I remember distinctly the Redevelopment Agency board's first reaction to the council's suggestion. "They can't make us build the park," the board members assured themselves (this was true). "If they won't let us build the bridge, then we won't build the park either, since it doesn't make sense to build a park no one can get to." I could understand (in part because I shared) the board's frustration, and I could appreciate the logic of their position, but because of the way the situation looked from the perspective of the mayor's office, I urged the board members to take a different approach. What I suggested when the council said no to the bridge was that the Redevelopment Agency should go ahead with the design and construction of the park and also complete as many of the missing segments of the riverfront trail as possible. It seemed to me that the bridge was something that could not be built (if it ever were to be built) until its time had come, and that its ripening would depend on the changing scene of the downtown riverfront. I concluded that the more complete the riverfront trail loop became, the more perturbing the remaining gaps would be, and that the more people there were using the trails, the more politically palpable that agitation would become. I thought the same about the bridge, and therefore, after listening sympathetically to the MRA board's frustration, I argued that the board should continue filling in the gaps in the trail and turn the wasteland of dirt piles in the shadow of the Orange Street Bridge into as attractive a park as possible, on the assumption that trails and parks across the river from each other would bring the need for the bridge into focus in a way that most people could not yet recognize.

The board did not readily (and some of its members did not ever) shift to the course I among others now urged on them. In part this reluctance arose from the perception — quite an accurate one — that if the need for the bridge were to emerge from the changes occurring on the riverfront, rather than from their own judgment and decision, the bridge might locate itself somewhere other than where they had already decided it should be. In particular, some board members could imagine that several improvements on both sides of the river just downstream from the Orange Street Bridge might make a footbridge more attractive over there, instead of upstream of Orange Street, where they had decided they wanted the bridge. I shared a certain amount of that trepidation, but I also came to see that we were better off letting the changing city itself locate the bridge than to bow our necks in defense of a particular location.

I might have liked a bridge as well as a park to show off to visitors, but for now I was content to let the evolving city sort out in its own terms and its own good time the issue of where its next bridge should stand. There may have been a time when I would have felt that my job as a politician was to push for a decision about the bridge location, and to see that the decision was implemented. In fact, I had done just that with the park, insisting that the process of deciding what kind of park we wanted not get bogged down, and then, once the decision was made, keeping the pressure on to get the dirt piles moved, the trees planted, and the paths laid. Clearly there is, and probably always will be, a place for such acts of will in the politician's trade. But about the bridge I felt differently, and as I explained my view to Mayor Schuster, he referred to the example of our sister city relationship to confirm my intuition that beyond the politician's risk-taking acts of will lay another dimension of politics which the city alone can teach.

Speaking of his strong belief that the sister city relationship was a good thing for Neckargemünd, the mayor acknowledged that he probably could have pushed the idea through his city council by an exercise of his own will. But the very point of being sister cities was to give a broad range of our citizens a chance to experience direct contact with the other city and another culture. This objective was more likely to be achieved if different sectors of each city came to value the exchange in their own terms. Oskar described for me, then, the difference between the type of politics that might have been reflected in a simple act of will and the type he chose to practice instead in this situation. As he spoke, I heard a theme I had by then encountered in stories from dozens of other city leaders from communities all across America. "I saw that we needed to take plenty of time with this decision about an American sister city," Mayor Schuster told me. "We needed to have many conversations, many chances for people to talk with each other about their concerns and apprehensions, and also about their different ways of seeing the possibilities. We had to find a way not just to persuade people that it was a good idea, but to get them to help shape it."

The gentle process of persuasion was, of course, part of his strategy to make sure I spent some time with members of the Green Party, and for my part I was glad to see it working. For my own political reasons, I wanted the sister city relationship to be one in which the two communities could learn from each other about recycling, about preserving open spaces, about protecting water quality. And beyond these arenas for education, Oskar and I, our council members, and our citizens were also learning from each other something new about the practice of politics.

Whatever the political issue — whether building a bridge or a sister city relationship — politics means and always will mean a risking of someone's political capital. This is unavoidable, and in a time of deepening political cynicism, it is made

riskier yet by a growing presumption that whatever a politician pursues is almost certainly tainted by a seeking of personal gain. Ironically, the impersonal, mechanical means upon
which we have come to rely so heavily to keep politics safe
only seem to deepen the cynicism. But now, from another
quarter, comes a very different influence upon politics. That
quarter is the living city, and it exercises its influence both
subtly and powerfully.

If, as Machiavelli argued, the greatest risk encountered by
political entrepreneurs comes from the influence of *Fortuna*
— from the unpredictable unfolding of the forces at work in
the world — then one mark of the good politician is knowing
when to let the world work, and when to work on the world.
To the extent that the world remains abstract and impersonal,
these risks remain immense, and in many cases incalculable:
only those persons with egos and wills to match such a magnitude of uncertainty are likely to engage those risks by becoming politicians. But to say that a city is organic is to recognize
that it *organ*izes in its own terms a certain portion of the world.
The city, in sound evolutionary fashion, shapes and organizes
itself entrepreneurially, ceaselessly risking and experimenting
with its possibilities. And the politician who learns to work
with the city begins to see opportunities to share risk-taking
with the city itself. So Oskar encouraged me to let the city
determine when and where the bridge would be built, as he
had let a long series of conversations determine when and in
what shape the sister city relationship would emerge.

As it turned out, our work had already taught me about one
of the world's most famous bridges, which in turn led me to
think of the siting of bridges in a way I might never have done
otherwise. Years before I ever visited Neckargemünd, I had in
a sense visited the Neckar, thanks to an elegant little essay of
Martin Heidegger's entitled "Building Dwelling Thinking."

Describing how the act of building, when it is thoughtfully done, gathers the world around itself and discloses that world to itself, Heidegger chooses as an illustration the old bridge Die Alte Brücke, across the Neckar in Heidelberg. On my first visit to Neckargemünd, I took Heidegger's essay with me, made the half-hour journey from Neckargemünd down the Neckar to Heidelberg, walked over the ancient bridge to the Philosopher's Walk up the mountain behind it, and from that vantage read anew Heidegger's description of the bridge below me:

> The bridge swings over the stream "with ease and power." It does not just connect banks that are already here. . . . With the banks, the bridge brings to the stream the one and the other expanse of the landscape lying behind them. It brings stream and bank and land into each other's neighborhood. The bridge gathers the earth as landscape around the stream.
>
> The location is not already there before the bridge is. Before the bridge stands, there are of course many spots along the stream that can be occupied by something. One of them proves to be a location, and does so because of the bridge. Thus the bridge does not first come to a location to stand in it; rather, a location comes into existence only by virtue of the bridge.[5]

The subtlety of Heidegger's prose may seem hopelessly at odds with the raw explicitness of so much of our politics. But it may also be that politics can only claim its human potential by becoming more comfortable with such subtlety, and even such paradox as Heidegger presents. To say, for example, that "the location is not already there before the bridge is" may seem like nonsense. But if the city is constantly responding to what it has already created and to what fortune brings forward, then the next act of creation must always be some paradoxical blend of will and acceptance.

This blend is precisely the defining characteristic of the good politician; it is Lorenzo, brooding, waiting for the moment of action, the moment when, of the "many spots along the stream that can be occupied by something . . . one of them proves to be a location, and does so because of the bridge." And because there are many moments when action might occur, the one for which Lorenzo waits proves to be the one in which political will may effectively be risked. This is the image Rumi evoked in a Middle Eastern city seven hundred years ago:

> In this town somewhere there sits a calm, intelligent man,
>   who doesn't know what he's about to do![6]

Like Lorenzo, Rumi's waiting figure is surrounded by the city, and it is the city, in its slow movement of unfolding, which prepares both the place and the time for its next (risky and uncertain) step in the direction of its own possibility. In fact, it is this possibility, which Lorenzo and Florence await together, which is the true meaning of politics as "the art of the possible."

As the organic nature of cities becomes more palpable in the variety of ways that this book has explored, more politicians find themselves willing to share their risk-taking with their cities and with their citizens. In the process, the entrepreneurship of power, never far from what politics must always be, becomes less self-centered; more politicians come to see it not as a zero-sum game where whatever power you have is power I lack, but instead as an expanding sum, where by investing well or risking wisely together, the whole city can grow stronger, healthier, and in every sense more prosperous.

At National League of Cities meetings, and anywhere else city leaders gather to learn from each other, it is obvious that these changes are beginning to attract into politics more and more people who take pleasure in sharing power as they share the inevitable risks of politics with a broader range of citizens.

JoAnn Yukimura, former mayor of the island of Kauai, Hawaii, entered politics as an outspoken advocate of a fairly narrow ideology (in her case, resistance to new developments on Kauai), but could not acquire the power to be effective until she had risked some of her hard-core ideological support in favor of a broader and less predictable political base. Her old friends were not altogether comfortable with her efforts to establish a broader consensus by listening more closely to their old enemies, while those traditional adversaries were always concerned that she might be "taking them for a ride."

This is the classic double-edged risk any politician faces when attempting to move toward a more consensus-based politics. In Yukimura's case, the risk was compounded by an implacable Machiavellian stroke of fortune, Hurricane Iniki, which devastated Kauai. Mayor Yukimura, encouraging citizens to get involved in solving the problems of the storm's aftermath instead of simply waiting for a governmental fix, risked a certain amount of credibility among those who were looking for simple, painless, technical solutions to the problems.

The gamble Yukimura took may have contributed to her narrow defeat in the next election, but her dignified response to that defeat is an example of how a politician's risk-taking can be understood as a stewardship of the community's own power. Reminding her disappointed supporters that the people of Kauai had in fact spoken at the election, Yukimura asked them to do whatever they could to help her successor do a good job of governing. This is power-sharing and power stewardship of the highest order — a commitment to good politics which had characterized Yukimura's approach to power. It is important to recognize that Yukimura was consistent in her approach to power from the beginning. She tried to teach her ideological compatriots that their island's welfare depended upon their learning to share decision-making with their old adversaries; she insisted that the healing of the island after the hurricane be carried out not just by city hall but by the whole island. And now, having perhaps paid a price for these risks, she insisted once again that the island gather its power and invest it in the new mayor so that he would have the best possible opportunity to govern the island well.

Visiting with her a few short weeks after the election, I could still read the hurt and disappointment in her face, and as one who had once lost a hard election himself, I understood what she confessed as her inclination to join her supporters in withholding assistance from her opponent. But Yukimura believed her earlier risk-taking had been well placed; she believed it had strengthened the island's political culture, and she was not about to wipe out those gains now by an act of self-indulgence. "I will be back," she told me, "and when I come back, I want to step into a working relationship with a more self-confident, more capable citizenry. The best way to do that is to help them have the experience of carrying the lessons we have learned together into this new administration."

The growing cadre of local leaders like JoAnn Yukimura who are intent on developing more collaborative leadership styles represents a crucial feature of the renaissance of the city. The trend is well established and will not be reversed, but neither will it replace overnight the prevailing zero-sum, top-down form of politics. There will continue to be politicians who serve too much their own interests or the interests of a narrow but powerful slice of their cities. Those who love to loathe politics, then, will continue to find in city hall plenty of grist for their cynical mill. But those whose love of their cities is even more potent than their hatred of politics might notice that cities pay more attention to their citizens' health as they become more aware of their own wholeness, and as this awareness leads to greater attention to their own children, so too does the city's emerging wholeness produce a richer and far more humanly satisfying practice of the indispensable art of politics.

To say that this kind of politics is more humanly satisfying is to acknowledge that such politics is a genuinely human enterprise — which means that it will always carry the flaws and imperfections embedded in the human condition. We will not get better politicians until we stop holding politics to a standard that no human enterprise can meet. Lorenzo's broken nose reminds us that the good politician is always just exactly the good enough politician. In fact, politicians will not be given the space to fulfill their human potential until their constituents, embracing their own potential imbedded in their own imperfections, take on the challenge of becoming good enough citizens.

EIGHT

The Good Citizen

One who is without a polis ... is either a poor sort of being, or a being higher than humans; he is like the person of whom Homer wrote in denunciation: "Clanless and lawless and heartless is he."

— ARISTOTLE, *Politics*

We do not say that a person who takes no interest in politics is one who minds his own business; we say that he has no business here at all.

— PERICLES, *Funeral Oration*

When the Crow people want to say that they are "lonely," they use a word which literally means, "I do not look like myself."

— From the film *Contrary Warriors*

I HAVE SOMETIMES FELT a brief but sharp pang of loneliness when I realize that someone I very much like or admire cannot quite grasp what I find so appealing about politics. Often enough these friends will say how grateful they are for the fact that I am willing to put up with the trials and frustrations of political life, but they always hasten to add that they could not do it themselves. And in fact, most of the time, they stay as far away from public life as possible, leaving the field to

a handful of professional or amateur politicians and a somewhat larger handful of what might be called professional citizens — regular performers at city council meetings or public
hearings. But all too often the people I most enjoy spending
time with, people in whom I have found a promising depth of
heart and soul, keep their distance from public life, which can
in turn only put distance between us and leave me with those
familiar thrusts of loneliness.

Of course, this emotion neither is nor deserves to be a
matter of general concern. But that which causes it — the distan-
cing of my friends and millions like them from public life — is
a matter of some importance to any democratic culture, and I
can at least thank these incidents of loneliness for teaching me
one human dimension of the issue.

Within the same arena, but at the other end of the emotional
scale, I find that one of the profound satisfactions of my job is
that it puts me in touch with so many people who, in an
astonishing variety of ways, put their hearts and all the wisdom they can bring to bear into projects and plans for improving one or another dimension of their community. The rich
texture created by the interlacing of these undertakings is no
small part of the transformation that, building upon its own
momentum, can turn an otherwise ordinary city into what
might come to be known and remembered as a good city. Even
beyond the concrete results of their work, these people have a
searing passion for their pet projects that is a great public
benefit; it offers a glimpse at a human potential for good work
that always makes me think, "There must be far more where
this comes from, if only we could encourage a little more and
stifle a little less of it."

But, as is the case with my apolitical friends, most of these
people are held at bay by public life itself, so that the passion
and wisdom they bring to particular projects rarely carry over

to what we might imagine as a full-bodied practice of citizenship. Yet only the development and the widening practice of such citizenship could bridge the gap I feel between myself and so many of my friends. The point of bridging that gap would not, of course, be to make me and other politicians feel less isolated. The value of a deepening practice of citizenship lies in the mutual healing and strengthening it would bring (and in fact is bringing) both to cities and to their citizens.

The stories of these small acts of healing are so numerous and so widespread that no city, no tiny village, would fail to discover its own collection of stories if it took the time to look. And it is worth taking the time. It is just in these simple stories, so clearly within the reach of every community and each of its members, that the teaching is available that could revive citizenship in its full potential to in turn revive the human potential of cities. Every community can begin to learn from its own stock of such stories, and if I offer one or two from Missoula, it is only to encourage the search for similar experiences elsewhere.

When my friends tell me that they could never do some of the things that I as a politician find myself doing, I often think they might have watched me enact a particular scene with which I have become all too familiar. One of the ways I have pursued my own understanding of Missoula's wholeness is through an aggressive (some might say ruthless) annexation policy. When I first ran for the city council, almost half of the sixty thousand people inhabiting the Missoula urban area actually lived within the city limits. The other half lived "in the county," in neighborhoods indistinguishable from "the city" except by the fact that their city neighbors paid for all the services and investments that enable a city to be a city. Those living "in the county" derived all the benefits of economy and culture that only a city can provide, and for which they chose to live right next to the city (which they might acknowledge in an unguarded moment), but for which they had so far not had the privilege of paying.

It happens that my tenure at city hall has coincided with a substantial shift in this state of affairs. A series of major annexations has increased the city's population by more than 50 percent, and while most of them would have occurred under anyone who happened to be mayor just at this time, I have steadfastly if not stubbornly nudged the annexations forward, a stance that has put me time and again in what my friends have come to call my Daniel in the Lion's Den role.

The scene for this little drama is always a junior high school gymnasium. The mayor and a few of his stalwart department heads sit at a table on the gym floor. One entire wall of bleachers seethes with "county residents" who have come to express their opinions about annexation. At some point during the evening, to insure that those opinions are in fact expressed, someone, in the name of democracy, will ask if everyone who wants to be annexed would please stand up. When, to all our amazement, no one stands, this champion of democracy will turn to me with an expression of mingled rectitude and contempt, which I should by now know better than to engage. Perhaps to my credit, I do not succumb to the temptation to suggest that the question is a little like asking if everyone who wants to be lynched by his neighbors would please stand up. I do not even offer the argument that if you ask people whether or not they would like to keep getting something for nothing, or whether they would like to join their neighbors in being taxed for it, you can be pretty sure what the answer will be. What I do say, sometimes, is that perhaps the truly democratic approach would be to draw a line around what looks from an aerial view to be the city, and then let everyone who lives inside the line vote on whether to be a city or not. There is in this argument enough logic (or at least enough of the kind of logic you would expect from a mayor) to slow the city-bashing temporarily, but it will soon be back up to full volume, and the mayor will once again be its personified target.

Of all the insults I have fielded in these scenes (or allowed to bounce into the stands for a ground rule double) the one that has haunted me the longest occurred during the early stages of our third major annexation, the Reserve Street Corridor. From my seat on the gym floor, I had listened to a hostile inquiry about what the questioner saw as the city's hopelessly inadequate snow removal procedures, and had given what I thought was a balanced and fair enough answer. My questioner, though, stepped back up to the microphone, and with a sneer you could spread on a cracker, asked, "Now would you please turn your head so we can see your other face?" I was, his tone reminded us all, a politician; worse, I was from the city: I had, then, to be lying. And the beauty of it was that nothing I could say would do anything but confirm that logic, since my words would still be the words of a shifty politician, so that the more convincing they might seem, the less they should be trusted.

At the end of that meeting, we asked members of the audience to sign up for one of several committees to help the city address issues of zoning and land use, police and fire protection, sewer extensions and park planning — issues that would have to be faced with or without their help if the annexation was in fact going to occur. Having witnessed the city's determination and ultimate success in two earlier annexations, several members of the crowd decided to at least hedge their bets by trying to make this annexation as palatable as possible. Over the next few weeks, they outlined the issues, organized their committees, and elected people to chair them who then met with me and our city staff to plan the next public meeting.

Still hearing echoes of the "turn your head" remark, I suggested that the committee chairs, all from the area to be annexed, take on the job of running the next meeting. Their first response was astonished silence, followed by a clamor of universal rejection. This annexation, they reminded us, was our idea, not theirs, and they were not about to take this burden from my shoulders. I persisted, though, arguing that if their efforts to make the annexation work better for the neighborhood were going to gain broader legitimacy, we needed meetings that moved beyond city-bashing to the kind of engagement with the issues that they and their committees had already achieved. Finally, one of the hardest-bitten of all the anti-annexation champions turned to her colleagues and said, ''I hate to say it, but the mayor is right: if we want this meeting to be anything but a gripe and whine session, we're going to have to run it ourselves.''

Which is what they did, sitting with us now on the gym floor, making it clear to their puzzled neighbors that they were still as opposed to annexation as ever, but that they thought the neighborhood should see our bet (or call our bluff) about making the annexation more palatable. They went out of their way to explain that, while they still disagreed with me about the annexation itself, the purpose of the meeting was not to trash the mayor, but to work on the issues.

None of these people had run such a large meeting before, and their neighbors, sensing this, tried to help them, at least on that score, to succeed. In deference to the committee chairs' courage in taking on this task, their neighbors began paying closer attention and asking more germane and constructive questions than in the first meeting. When one still angry resident, trying to rouse resentment against city taxes, asked how much of their tax increase would be going to the mayor's salary, several people sitting near him groaned, and one man shouted from the other end of the bleachers, ''That's not what we're here for!" When another self-described "taxpayer" complained about the city's propensity to waste money on nonsense such as riverfront parks and trails, I decided to appeal to the audience's pride in their city by describing how most Missoulians enjoyed showing off our riverfront to visitors, or taking them to Out to Lunch at Caras Park. Winding up with an unabashedly chauvinistic challenge to any other city in the region to match the charm of Missoula's riverfront, I was greeted, for the first time ever in one of these meetings, with a vigorous round of applause.

This applause for a mayor who had expressed these folks' own feeling of pride in their city was, it seemed to me, a fairly complex act of citizenship. The sense of pride in a well-loved part of the city was indispensable to this moment of citizenship. But there was something more than this in their applause: all of us in that gymnasium felt that there was in that moment something new, something that had never existed in one of these meetings before, and that this new thing had actually been gathering force throughout the evening. It surfaced in applause because a number of people had made a split-second decision to move beyond their familiar and comfortable posture of resentment and anger into at least a momentary stance of affirmation. However tentative the new posture might be, it had required a fair degree of courage on the part of all those who had joined in the applause, since those sitting next to them would very likely resent this departure from the solidarity of shared resentment. I could not help feeling that, mixed in with their expression of pride in Missoula, was an element of pride in themselves, an unspoken acknowledgment to one another that they carried within themselves the capacity to do the right thing, even if the right thing was just at this moment something as difficult as applauding what the mayor had said. But by this time the mayor had become more than a little secondary to the situation, and no one was happier about that than the mayor himself.

In an unexpected way, either the balance of power or the center of gravity had shifted substantially away from me at the very moment several members of the audience told their angry neighbor that my salary was not what they were there to talk about. By deflecting that form of criticism from me, they knew that they risked strengthening my hand in terms of what they had seen until now as a mere power struggle. But in fact, by claiming a kind of moral high ground, they had shifted authority away from the officials onto themselves, and when, a few minutes later, they applauded my remarks, it was from that position of moral authority that they did so. The stage for this shift had been set by the committee chairs when they decided to risk their own standing in their neighborhood by running the meeting. This was an act of courage, and their neighbors responded first with respect, and then with a positive response to the committee chairs' call for civility in the conduct of the meeting. And it was because they had made this implicit promise of civility that a number of what would otherwise have been angry "taxpayers" were able to take on the role of citizens as the meeting progressed. It was precisely when members of the audience took responsibility for the civility of the meeting that citizenship claimed its authority, and that the mayor and other officials could assume what I would argue is their own more modest and appropriate role.

The degree of civility that this handful of people brought to bear on this particular meeting may seem trivial compared to the intractability of the problems faced by most cities. In fact, I suspect that most of the people who enforced civility in that setting would minimize its significance compared to the "real" issues of sewer extension costs, snow removal, and fire protection that they had come there to talk about. But for my part, I would not trade that moment of "That's not what we're here to talk about!" for all the technical fixes I have ever encountered. If every meeting that dealt with a difficult public issue could, by its own dynamic, produce a half-dozen people who took upon themselves some measure of responsibility for the way people treated each other, we would solve problems at a much higher rate than most of us in most of our cities have ever experienced.

The reason is that civility is the genius of the city. Like politics or business, civility is one of those words that has lost most of its depth: we now think of civility as a simple matter of manners. It is, indeed, a matter of manners, but there is nothing simple about it. Just as "politics" springs from the Greek name for the city-state, "civil," "civility," "civilization," and "citizenship" all derive from the Roman word for "city." Living together in a city is challenging; it requires a special way of relating to one another, and that way of relating is called civility. But as cities, across the millennia, have acquired an organic life force of their own, civility has broadened beyond a pure survival mechanism to something more akin to a life instinct, and like the biological instinct for life, which is not always content with mere survival, the life instinct of the city turns its energy to the pursuit and realization of opportunities for the city to thrive and prosper. It is when civility makes this turn that civilization emerges. Whenever in the course of history the organic life force of cities is again recognized and nurtured, a rebirth of the vital strands of civilization will result. In those terms, then, civility is no trivial matter, and any mayor might well do more than sigh with relief at the sign of its reemergence. The good politician knows that no amount of political leadership can replace the benefits of that kind of citizenship.

Before he became mayor of Pasadena, Rick Cole had been

involved in a deeply adversarial land-use planning controversy, which eventually tied up the entire town in a prolonged
lawsuit. When Cole became mayor, he and his vice mayor,
Katie Mack (who had been on the opposite side of the controversy from Cole) agreed that this approach was not serving
anyone's interests very well, and certainly was not serving
Pasadena well. As Cole puts it, he and Mack "banged the
heads" of their respective sets of allies to reach consensus on
the land-use issues that had so divided the community.

In fact, what Cole and Mack did was to call a number of
people to citizenship, and the result was a multilayered civilizing of the community. Cole speaks of bringing "nonzealots"
into the land-use discussion "who had a moderating influence
on the zealots on both sides." Acknowledging that he himself had been one of the zealots resisting the city's growth,
Cole describes how his allies and supporters, in order to be
heard by ordinary citizens, began prefacing their comments
with phrases such as, "We've never been against all growth,
but . . . ," while those who had led the countercharge began
saying, "We're not in favor of growth at any cost, but . . ."
Slowly, and then with more creativity and confidence, these
polarized Pasadenans began speaking in a language their op-
ponents could hear.

Perhaps no skill is more important to the office of citizen
than the ability to teach or encourage one another to speak so
that you can actually be heard by others who do not already
share your views. One of the great signs of the periodic weakening of democratic culture is the tendency to fall into one or
both of two kinds of self-indulgence: to speak always and
everywhere in chorus with those who share the same views, or
to fall into complaint, whining, and anger. Many of the talk
radio hosts of the nineties are simply parasites on these worst

and lowest instincts, this fundamental alienation of people from their democratic competence.

Meanwhile, Rick Cole and Katie Mack and thousands like them in large and small cities everywhere lead a quiet, modest, but desperately needed and deeply powerful movement in the other direction. Refusing to let people indulge themselves in the sullen self-pity that feeds the radio talk shows, leaders like Cole distinguish between input and genuine democratic citizenship. "We don't need your input," Cole sometimes tells citizens, or people about to become citizens. "We need your help in solving problems."

When citizens meet that challenge, civility — the crucial first step of teaching one another to speak in order to be heard — can move on to the work of civilization, not as a historical abstraction, but as the realization of the city's potential in the most concrete terms. As the Pasadena land-use discussion grew less heated, less a matter of scoring points than of solving problems, the process of framing issues grew steadily more productive. Cole describes how, under the influence of the "nonzealots," the slogan-slinging of the progrowth and antigrowth camps "moved from a useless, never-ending debate about the quantity of growth to a constructive conversation about targeted growth."

At the same time, the role of the automobile in land-use issues came under closer scrutiny. "As folks became more comfortable with each other, they started talking about the mobility of people, about where they needed to go and why, rather than talking past each other about the circulation of traffic as either an unquestioned good or an unquestioned evil in itself," Cole said. He describes how these changes in language and emphasis led to a gradual shifting of political alliances. "Environmentalists, who had previously lined up in the slow-or-no-growth camp, now began to support targeted, higher-density development because they had been persuaded that only that kind of development could sustain a public transportation system."

As the conversation became more civil, then, it became more capable of problem solving, which led in turn to a more productive attention to what could be done to make the city work well. But we need to resist, on two different fronts, the temptation to see this merely as a response to a technical problem. The clustering of higher-density developments, which could protect open space while enabling Pasadena's transportation system to work better, was a good example of collaborative problem solving; however, we miss its true significance if we regard it as the deployment of a particular kind of problem-solving technique (collaboration) in search of an equally technical solution to a particular land-use problem (clustering). What we leave out is the role of the city itself both in shaping the solution and heightening the satisfaction of all parties.

Development patterns that create attractive living space while improving the transportation system are exactly the sort of "structures of wholeness" out of which the city's own wholeness will emerge. As citizens become more practiced at working together with the city's best interests at heart, it is precisely such structures of wholeness that recommend themselves to their attention. And it is here that we begin to see how the city itself continues to be present in — and to pursue its own interests through — the nurture and practice of civility.

When Rick Cole and Katie Mack and their respective camps of land-use partisans began prefacing their remarks with phrases like "We've never been against all growth, but . . . ," they were extending a verbal hand to one another, a more open hand than the fistlike attack slogans that had taken them to court against each other. In that sense, their new lead-in lines sound like civility as mere politeness. Such politeness is indispensable to moving from an adversarial to a problem-solving stance, but it was something more than politeness that, centuries ago, drew the word "civility" from the word "city." If it were possible for the city of Pasadena to have expressed its own opinion about growth and development, it would almost certainly have used language more like what the citizens *learned* to use than what they began by using. The city would use such language not to be polite but to express the complexity of its own organic condition.

We are reminded again of Jane Jacobs's description of a city as "a problem in organized complexity." Rarely would a city, attempting to respond to such organic complexity, choose to be as static or as heedless as the antigrowth or pro-growth slogans would trap it into being. The language of tempered change that Pasadenans taught themselves was much more nearly the language of the city, then, not in form alone, but also in the substance of what was being said. With the assistance of that language, the various factions could begin to solve problems — "problems of organized complexity" — instead of simply trying to win arguments. The solutions that began to emerge were the city's own solutions, its way of drawing nearer to its own wholeness. In just this way, in hundreds of settings every day, cities use the movement toward civility in the service of civilization.

One of the more promising developments in this arena has been the recent emergence of a movement that has been variously entitled "public journalism" or "civic journalism." Led by newspapers like the *Wichita Eagle* and the *Charlotte Observer*, this new approach to journalism has been openly entrepreneurial in its approach. Recognizing that the effortless accessibility of the electronic media is now a serious threat to the viability of print journalism, a growing number of publishers, with their eyes steadily fixed on the bottom line, have begun proving that something quite different than the USA Today "TV on newsprint" approach may actually sell newspapers. The National Civic League describes how these pioneering newspapers, by remembering the traditional role of the press in a genuinely democratic society, are generating new markets for themselves:

> After all, they theorized, journalists are chroniclers of civic life. If the citizens of a community withdraw from the public arena — from the give and take of the marketplace of ideas — leaving it to the politicians and the single-issue groups, then the need for journalism in all its forms is diminished.[1]

In other words, a healthy civic life, where people actually have some reason to read newspapers, may provide the best market conditions in which a newspaper can operate. Based on this hypothesis, those publishers who have embraced civic journalism do nothing more than make themselves the best vehicles for genuine public discourse that they know how to be. If people decide that they need newspapers (and other forms of media that are joining the movement) to shape and direct their communities, then newspapers that fill that need in a legitimate way will find themselves being read — having first, of course, been purchased (or otherwise sustained).

So, for example, the Charlotte Observer, along with the local ABC affiliate and two local radio stations, sponsored neighborhood meetings on issues of crime and violence, after carefully providing the best information available on how those problems affected Charlotte's neighborhoods. People read the newspapers, listened to the radio, and watched TV in advance of the meetings, participated more intelligently in the meetings, and then read about their discussions (and those of other neighborhoods) in the follow-up stories.

In Tallahassee, Florida, the *Tallahassee Democrat*, a TV station, and two local colleges conducted a series of focus groups to determine what issues mattered most to Tallahassee citizens. The newspaper then ran surveys on the issues identified, published the results on the front page, and advertised a public forum to discuss those issues. The TV station and the newspaper agreed in advance to give prime coverage to the forum. Ed Fouhy wrote:

> What's the goal of this project? In the words of *Tallahassee Democrat* editor Lou Heldman, it is to achieve Daniel Yankelovich's "state of highly developed public opinion that exists once people have engaged an issue, considered it from all sides, understood the choices it leads to and accepted the full consequences of the choices they make."[2]

In a variety of ways, determined both by the entrepreneurial instincts of the media operators and the needs of the community, the exploration of this newly rediscovered role of journalism has steadily gathered momentum. The *Boston Globe*, the *Seattle Times*, the *Dallas Morning News*, and the *San Francisco Chronicle* are among the newspapers leading the foray into an arena in which cities learn once again what it is to deal with issues in a genuinely democratic way. Creating controversy for the sake of controversy was never the best way to run a city, and as more publishers decide that it may not be the best way to run a newspaper, either, more citizens are being given tools with which to shift from a stance of anger, alienation, or narrow self-interest to a more civil posture.

This shift, the same one that occurred on the gym floor in Missoula, is the crucial moment in the evolution of citizenship.

It is when citizenship assumes this stance and this voice that democracy itself becomes not a mere slogan, but an important and deeply satisfying human enterprise. In fact, it is just this shift from an adversarial to a problem-solving stance that seems to have enabled democracy to take root and survive as a historical phenomenon.

I once heard someone describe what had enabled Athens to make its democratic experiment viable enough for a long enough period that history has never forgotten the lesson. It was not, this student of Athens said, because Athenians agreed about everything; even the relatively narrow circle of those admitted to citizenship disagreed fiercely about all kinds of issues, both domestic and foreign. Rather, democracy took root and flourished in Athens because, on most issues, citizens taught themselves to act and speak "as if they cared more about Athens than they cared about winning."

This care is what gives genuine democratic discourse its special flavor; it is what brings the city and the voice of the city into the discourse; it is what makes civility not only a social but a political phenomenon. And here I should correct what I have said earlier, when I argued that civility is more than a matter of politeness. Having moved from Rome to Athens, it is obvious now that just as the city, the *civis*, stands behind and speaks through civility, so does the city-state, the polis, speak through politeness, one of a score of words (from politics to police) that we have drawn from that unforgettable Athenian experiment with democracy. What we have all too much forgotten is how fundamentally humanistic, how much in the service of the good life, that experiment was and still remains.

We are now so accustomed to seeking personal wholeness through various forms of self-development, counseling, or therapy that it would occur to very few people to think of citizenship as a path to greater individual wholeness. We may find it curious, but probably still largely irrelevant, that there have been times, not least the time of the birth of Athenian democracy, when most of the people who thought and wrote about human wholeness concluded that no one could be a whole human being, nor achieve the satisfactions of such wholeness, without participating fully in citizenship. We are, fortunately, catching glimpses again of that ancient wisdom in the steadily growing appreciation for the concept and experience of "community." Community is humanly satisfying because it engages so many sides and facets of us; it responds to and nurtures what we sense to be our innate or potential wholeness. But by itself, the concept of community falls at least two steps short of what the full-bodied revival of citizenship might offer.

The two steps may seem at first glance to run counter to each other. On the one hand, it may appear possible simply to enjoy community as a given, as a commodity, as something one might pay taxes for, and then have it delivered by professional community-builders, more or less the way the public water supply is delivered to each household by a corps of professionals. In fact, community cannot be delivered in that way because it is not such a commodity. The wisest of the communitarian theorists recognize that community cannot happen at all without a shouldering of responsibility by a wide variety of people who are not "service providers," but who must also learn to think of themselves as something besides service recipients (and, of course, taxpayers). Too seldom in the communitarian literature is this shouldering of responsibility given its full title, which is that of citizenship. Regardless of what it is called, the assumption of one's own responsibility for making community happen is its own reward. And as it is true that without this assumption of responsibility, community itself cannot occur on the outside of the person, it is equally true that without the more subjective experience of this engagement of responsibility, the human wholeness that community promises must also remain incomplete.

But if assuming individual responsibility for making community happen is a necessary element of community, there is also a sense in which we seem called upon to understand that we are not individually, or even as a collection of individuals, entirely responsible for the wholeness of our cities — the city carries that wholeness and the capacity for attaining it within itself. Even though the city must and will require our cooperation and assistance to realize its potential, still it shares that responsibility with us rather than expecting us to fulfill it entirely on our own.

It is, to say the least, a stretch, given our highly rationalistic and indeed mechanistic approach to public life, to imagine how a city could share with us the work of achieving its own fullness. It may seem more than sufficient to call upon people to shoulder such responsibility themselves; it may indeed seem counterproductive to offer to take some of the pressure off by suggesting some largely undefinable sharing of the burden with "the city itself." But if it seems paradoxical to argue that citizenship involves both a greater shouldering of individual responsibility and a kind of moderation in what we claim responsibility for, it is in just this paradox that some of the most humanizing work of the city occurs. To understand how that happens, we might revisit two themes introduced in earlier chapters: the concept of busyness and that of grace.

If busyness is of the very essence of the city, it is also one of the great curses of modern life. A city spins synergy from its busyness, but too many of its residents turn their individual share of that busyness into heart attacks, strokes, or alcoholism. Almost without exception, families that we would term successful by any standard economic measure would describe themselves as far too busy, trying to do too many things at once, knowing in whatever moments of deep honesty they might encounter that their busyness is making their lives less humanly satisfying than they should be. Yet this very busyness is what produces the synergy that makes cities prosperous and successful, confirming that the "business recruitment efforts" of such cities are really measured by the synergy-producing busyness they create.

Do cities, then, only prosper at the expense of the health and sanity of their citizens? That would be the reverse of the conclusion of the healthy cities movement, which is founded on the premise that the health of cities and of their residents are mutually dependent. And in fact, the healthy cities movement points to the path through this apparent paradox between the health-threatening busyness of individuals and the healthy economy that it promises.

The healthy cities movement only makes sense if we are prepared to acknowledge that cities are enough like organisms that we can actually speak of them as healthy or unhealthy. But the essence of organisms is that their wholeness cannot be captured by adding together all their parts. When individual cells evolve into an organism, something new emerges that cannot be described simply by adding together all the cells. This is precisely what is meant by the synergy of cities. The very concept of synergy is an affront to sharply analytical minds, because synergy cannot be located in any of the parts of what is being analyzed. But, of course, synergy means that something beyond the mere collection of individual activities has suddenly entered the picture. To say that a city is organic, then, and that healthy cities produce various kinds of synergy, is to say the same thing in two different ways.

If the city is organic, it must have (and indeed we can see that any good city does have) a life force of its own. But imagine for a moment an organism that, while blessed with such an organic vitality, was made up of cells that were unaware of the existence of that life force. Imagine that the cells felt called upon to supply, by their own exertions, the equivalent of that life force on behalf of the entire body. My political experience has left me convinced, and every day I become more strongly convinced, that our citizenship is too much like the existence of these hypothetically overstressed cells. We try too hard; we carry too much of the burden, because we do not recognize that the city in its organic wholeness has developed its own vital energy, its own life and its own capacity to sustain and enhance the good life for its citizens.

If we were to apply this way of thinking to the economic dimension of the city, it would lead to the conclusion that we are capable of greater prosperity at less cost, by many measures of cost, but certainly at less cost in terms of human overwork and stress. If it were possible to aggregate the number of hours humans work to produce income to pay for nonproductive or counterproductive activities, and then imagine instead a society and an economy in which we concentrated on producing only what is good for us rather than what does us harm, we would have created a picture where people doing less would get more from it. That promise, I am convinced, lies within the domain of the good city, and will be disclosed as we become more confident of the real meaning of the city's synergy. But for now, I will only contend that on the side of life I myself know best, the side of civic energy, this same dynamic is indeed true, and demonstrably so.

I have taken to arguing, at least among people I trust not willfully to misinterpret me, that Missoula would be better off if all its busiest citizens would set themselves the goal of doing half as much for the city as they now do. This largely whimsical but not altogether facetious suggestion rests on two related foundations. First, for everyone in the city who spends too many evenings away from the family working to improve the community, there are many more Missoulians whose lives would almost certainly be enriched if they felt encouraged to become more constructively involved in the life of the community. In fact, many of the worst problems the city faces, problems that hundreds of citizens overwork themselves trying to solve, are as much as anything the result of other hundreds of residents feeling ignored and alienated, and as a consequence resorting to a wide range of personally and socially destructive behaviors. A successful effort, therefore, to share the burdens and the satisfactions of citizenship more broadly will make some people more healthy by becoming less frantic, others more whole by becoming more engaged, and the city itself more robust as a result.

There is, then, a strong democratic argument to be made for the city's busiest citizens setting themselves the goal of doing less. But there is also another, far less easily quantified benefit, which will return us at last to the theme of grace. If indeed there is a wholeness toward which the good city strives, and if that wholeness must be comprised, as in any organism, by a healthy balance among various systems (in the case of the city, by an integration of the physical body of the city with its economy, its social structure, its culture), then every step in the direction of the city's healing is by definition a step toward the resolution of many of the problems with which so many citizens so valiantly struggle. Almost without exception, these people are engaged in one or another of those small acts of healing that contribute to the healing of the entire organism. I can imagine no picture of the good city in which people would not continue to be called to address themselves to such problems, bringing all their creativity and goodwill, as they now do, to the solution of those problems. But I can imagine a less anxious, less frantic way of approaching those challenges than we usually practice. If, with every problem we tackle, we could assume that the emerging wholeness of the city was our ally, it would add a quality to our citizenship that would, I am convinced, leave us feeling at once more relaxed and more confident of achieving what we had set out to do.

In sports of all kinds, we are familiar with just this "more relaxed and more confident" posture. Whether teeing off on the golf course or diving from the high board, the surest results are always attended by an elegant economy of effort. For this we have a name, and no other name will do: we call it grace. When Pericles reached the climax of his funeral oration, holding before his hearers in one supremely eloquent moment the essence of both the good city and the good citizen, he concluded that Athens had become "an education to Greece," and that "each single one of our citizens, in all the manifold aspects of life, is able to show himself the rightful lord and owner of his own person, and to do this, moreover, with exceptional grace." Such grace is still the surest mark of genuine citizenship because it reflects as nothing else can the full human potency of the citizen graced by the unfolding wholeness of the city itself.

I had become accustomed, at Farmers' Market, to watching the way people shared their delight in the market, and how, in that way, they had become steadily more at ease about sharing their delight at life in general. This, after all, is the real point: to live in a manner that we are able genuinely to enjoy, which has been the object of our labor, and which is the true bounty of the good city. But as I became convinced that Farmers' Market represented, in this sense, the city at its very best, I also noticed another dimension to it. Summers in Missoula are generally glorious, but all too short, and the winters seem to drag on forever. I have been known to annoy the chamber of commerce by quoting publicly the most irreverent description of Missoula's weather: "Nine months of winter and three months of bad skiing." For everyone in Missoula, these long winters are never far away, and as summer draws to a close, we all prepare ourselves, in our various individual ways, for the long darkness. It was this that I saw at the market: on clear September mornings, as squash and pumpkins began appearing in the booths, people would speak to each other of their regrets at the ending of summer, and it seemed to me that this made it easier for some of us at least to acknowledge our regrets about some of life's other inevitabilities.

Down at the other end of Higgins Avenue, I discussed all this with my friend at the season's last Out to Lunch at Caras Park. After we had spoken of our sadness at the end of this series of leisurely Wednesday meetings, we said goodbye, and I started back to my office while the music still played. My sadness mounted as I climbed the steps to the street level, and at the top I found myself turning not toward city hall, but out onto the Higgins Avenue Bridge, where I stood at the railing for several minutes, looking down at the crowd gathered at the amphitheater. I noticed how people stood in shifting clusters; I imagined some of the conversations they might be having, knowing as my friend and I had known that they would not be meeting here again for a long time. Above all, I was struck as I had been so often at the market, by the easy, relaxed way people carried themselves. The music seemed to contribute to that ease, creating a kind of languor in everyone's movements, a sense that there was time enough for one last conversation. I felt then that I had never appreciated the city so much, because it was clearly the city that had created this space within which people now stood and moved so gracefully. The more I allowed myself to appreciate how good life had become, the more I felt as well the sadness of the passing of the season. I knew then that this wonderfully productive, creative era in

Missoula's history would also someday come to an end, pass into something else, and that brought on an even deeper feeling of regret.

I became aware just then of someone leaning on the railing next to me, and turning, I noticed that during my reverie Ira Byock had joined me at the rail. I had known Ira and his family in many settings and from many different perspectives over our years together in Missoula, but mostly I knew Ira for his outstanding work as a hospice physician. He had helped us bring to Missoula the Chalice of Repose, a remarkable training program in the medieval art of using song and harp music to assist in life's final passage. Because of his widespread reputation, Ira had also been able to persuade the Academy of Hospice Physicians to hold its national convention, the following summer, in Missoula.

Always alert to synergies within the city, I suddenly realized that Ira was involved in developing a Missoula-centered synergy of another kind. As we visited on the bridge about the upcoming convention, I joked that, while I had always held Missoula up as a good place to live, I might have to start arguing that it was also becoming a good place to die. But then, looking back toward the shrinking last-of-the-season crowd in the amphitheater, it came to me that it was no joke at all. Here the city had cradled a place for the good life, but that could only finally be true if it were a place for the good life in all its human dimensions. Suddenly I thought once again of that other bridge, just downriver from our sister city, and of what it had inspired Heidegger to write: "Always and ever differently the bridge escorts the lingering and hastening ways of people to and fro, so that they may get to other banks and in the end, as mortals, to the other side."[3] Recalling myself then to this much more mundane bridge, I said goodbye to Ira and walked back to my work in the heart of the city.

Afterword

🎋

B ECAUSE THE MAYOR'S POSITION in Missoula is a full-
time job, this book was written on weekend mornings,
most of it over coffee or breakfast at one or another of the
downtown establishments, like the Shack or the Old Town
Cafe, where Missoulians perfect and embellish the art of wak-
ing up. I often found myself moved by the personal concern of
neighbors who, assuming I must be working on matters mayoral, would politely approach my table and urge me to take
some time off. Explaining that I was writing a book helped
some, but then when they inquired (as they often did) about
the title, they usually started worrying aloud that if I was
advertising Missoula as "the good city," I would just make
more people want to move here. I had to spend more time,
then, explaining that the book was about cities in general, and
that, if anything, I hoped that by encouraging people to improve their own cities, they would feel less inclined to move to
places like Missoula, places which have plenty of their own
problems, not least the problem of absorbing too many people
fleeing other problems in other cities.

Despite such interruptions, I did finally manage to finish
the manuscript and send it off, express mail, to the publisher. If
I ever had any doubts about whether I was really a writer, or
only a weekend hobbyist, my reaction to releasing my manuscript left me quite clear about the answer. It happened that I

was flying to Santa Fe the day I mailed the package. Delayed in Salt Lake City by an early winter blizzard in the Rockies, I arrived late in Santa Fe and had to eat dinner alone.

Worn out by both the final push to finish the book and the long day of fighting my way down the spine of the continent, I fell into a reverie while I waited for my food, and found myself, ridiculously enough, wondering not only whether my manuscript had arrived in New York, but how it was doing there. Where exactly might it be in the city? Whose hands had it passed through in the course of the day, and how had they treated it? Knowing that I would be traveling to New York in a few days myself, I found that I was looking forward to reconnecting with the book, but I also realized that by then it would be essentially on its own. Having sent children to college in cities unfamiliar to me, I had watched them form relationships to those cities, growing into themselves as they responded to their new surroundings. Restoring itself now with the unaccustomed but still western tastes and colors of Santa Fe, my tired mind allowed itself to imagine my book moving out into the world, thousands of miles away, in something like the same way my children had.

I had come to Santa Fe to meet with the other advisory board members from the Pew Partnership for Civic Change. Our work together, for the last two years, had been to review grant applications from dozens of midsize cities across the country, to select the dozen or so best proposals for furthering cooperation across race, class, and ideological lines for the betterment of these cities. At this meeting, we were to meet teams of elected officials and citizens from each of those cities, discussing with them the specifics of their city-building work and the common themes running through it.

Anyone who doubts that there is a powerful healing occurring in the body politic would have been hard-pressed to carry that skepticism unscathed from the discussion in Santa Fe. Over and over, in voices filled with passion and compassion, yet disciplined by years of hard experience, of trying and failing and getting up to try again, these politicians and citizens told the stories of the slow, incremental, but ever more self-sustaining healing of their cities.

More than once that weekend, I felt an urge to call my editor and ask him to send the manuscript back so I could get more of these stories into it. I had already written a little about Peoria's sidewalk-building program where construction workers served as mentors to potential gang members, and about Utica's effort to heal a neighborhood by rethinking the role of a medical center. But now it seemed that I should tell the story of Asheville, North Carolina. With a population of just over sixty thousand and an enviable unemployment rate of 3.3 percent, the city was nevertheless concerned about its city-region, where more than one quarter of the citizens lived in poverty. Asheville had decided to work with the surrounding small towns and their often impoverished artisans to establish the city-region as the "Center for Handmade in America."

And what about the two Charlestons in our group of grantees? Charleston, South Carolina, facing the possible closure of its naval base, was nevertheless calmly, confidently creating the Civic Forum on Families, committing every segment of the community to work together to strengthen the city's families. And Charleston, West Virginia, unwilling to leave the fate of its poorest families to state or federal debates over welfare reform, had established Family Resource Centers, which were designed to recapture the ancient meaning of the proverb "It takes a village to raise a child."

What does it mean that Fargo, North Dakota, and Moorhead, Minnesota, are reaching across the Red River that separates them, collaborating to address new racial and ethnic tensions as Hispanic migrant workers, Kurdish refugees, and Asians begin to change the complexion of towns that had until now resembled nothing so much as Lake Wobegon? What might other communities with longstanding racial and ethnic tensions learn from Santa Fe's broad-based collaboration, in the face of growth-induced escalation in housing prices, to preserve the affordability of housing for its large Hispanic population? What kind of change is afoot when Longview and Tyler, bitter Texan rivals separated by an oil field, respond to the decline in oil production by fashioning between them a series of "Developing Our People" community forums?

In the end, I decided to leave the body of the book alone and simply accept as a confirmation of its main themes the fact that cities, large and small, will continue to produce an ever growing list of stories of the healing of the body politic. The good citizens and politicians who had come to Santa Fe to share their stories deserve a book apiece, but as Pericles told the Athenian citizens whose work he so admired, the only appropriate memorial to their good work would be the future of the city itself. By the time I left Santa Fe, I was ready to let my book go its way, confident that my colleagues' city-healing work would only continue to underscore the message of hope this book has tried to convey.

But I found that my fatherly concerns about my book's encounter with the big city were still not entirely resolved. It was one thing to be confident in a setting like Santa Fe, but doesn't the picture look a whole lot different from a Manhattan perspective? As if to underline my concerns, I now discovered among my conference materials a cartoon that one of the organizers had included in the conference packets as a way of welcoming us to Santa Fe. It was a *New Yorker* cartoon, showing a man speaking earnestly to a companion at a table in a restaurant. The artwork on the restaurant wall clearly identified Santa Fe, but the humor was all New York. "I love Santa Fe," the man muses, "but only New York understands me." I loved Santa Fe, too, but I was far less certain about the New York part.

As it happened, I arrived in New York on election day, found my book well cared for by my editor, but, as I suspected, found it also gradually freeing itself from my control. The next morning I spent some time aimlessly walking the streets of Manhattan as the city absorbed the fact that, with Governor Mario Cuomo's defeat, it had lost a friend in the governor's office, and may now be more on its own with its own problems than years of solicitude from Albany had trained it to be. Nationwide, the 1994 election campaign had been more universally negative and nasty than any election in anyone's memory, and I almost expected to see an intensification of nastiness on these streets which most non–New Yorkers already stereotype as profoundly uncivil. But my experience was actually quite different.

I have never become anything but a stranger to the streets of Manhattan, jumping at every blast of a taxi's horn, hopelessly deploying what in Missoula would be politeness to fellow pedestrians, but which here only confuses and annoys those who stumble on my halting heels or dodge at the last second into the space I should have just vacated, but in which I had instead (politely) paused.

At Fifth and Forty-sixth I finally plant myself, safely and firmly, against the corner of a building, and simply attempt to sort out for a few minutes the pandemonium of the intersection before me. As I slowly absorb the intricacy of this dance of vehicles and humans, it dawns on me that what in Missoula would be taken as the grossest incivility is, at this intersection, nothing more or less than what it takes to make the city work. More than one or two instances of Missoulian leisureliness would quickly become, at such a spot, like sand in a well-oiled and well-timed machine. To call my way of moving "politeness" in such a setting would be as inappropriate as to call these New Yorkers' practiced movements "uncivil." Once again I was compelled, by the sheer vitality of this intersection, to remember that both "politeness" and "civility" were concepts drawn from the city or polis, and that this city at this and hundreds of other intersections had created just exactly what it took to make the city work. I also realized that, given a few weeks, the city would have begun, for my own good as well as its own, to "civilize" me.

The city did not, I knew, work as well as it should — but then, neither did mine. My experience in Santa Fe had, however, convinced me anew that the work of civilization had indeed entered a new period of vitality, and that both New York and Missoula would be the better for it. Was I imagining it, or hadn't I already encountered at the hotel desk, at a cafeteria, and in a dozen or so other spots around the city a degree of civility I had not expected?

What made me think I was not imagining it was a stop I had made earlier that morning farther down the island. My meanderings then had brought me to Union Square, and to the outdoor market that occupied the square. Suddenly my experience of the city shifted from taxis and crazily careening bicycles to fresh bread and bagels, cut flowers, cheeses, and vegetables. Wandering among the booths and tables, watching the natives inspecting the goods with an eye for local nuances I could only guess at, I recalled how often, in markets from Neckargemünd to Sapporo, I had received one more lesson in the deeper meaning of local culture. Now I was reminded specifically of an earlier journey to upstate New York, where I had learned how the revival of farmers' markets in New York

City was slowly remaking and strengthening the farm economy of the city's hinterlands.

Most of the shoppers here at Union Square were not, I
suspected, thinking about the farmers who depended upon
them buying a braid of garlic or a slab of cheese. But many of
them were aware of their own and their families' health, and of
how their purchases of fresh bread, cheese, or produce might
contribute to it. What it was perhaps easier for an outsider to
see was that the city, by providing this opportunity for the
pursuit of individual health, had also made the city itself marginally healthier.

The city's more integrated relationship to its larger region
was one element of this greater wholeness. In addition to that,
the city, by repairing and refurbishing the old square, had
reclaimed a significant "structure of wholeness" that must
already be reaching healing fingers into the entire neighborhood surrounding it. The solace of this bit of occupied open
space, and the subtly civilizing effect of its leisurely, face-to-
face exchanges could only, over time, make the surrounding
offices better places to work, simply because there was a civilized place nearby for workers to repair to, and then to bring
some of its freshness and openness back with them to the
workplace.

The renovation of the square was still underway, complete
with the traditional construction site notice of what the city
was up to here, and why. Knowing how overwhelmed the
city's budgets always were by the impossible press of social
problems, I could only imagine how often someone must have
growled, "What are they doing spending this kind of money
on frills when they can't even . . . ," the "they can't even" list
being inexaustible in its variety and urgency. Yet in spite of
such sniping and second-guessing, some politicians had made

the decision to invest a portion of the city's sorely pressed resources in this small but potent act of healing.

Scanning the construction announcement, I came upon the name of Ruth Messenger, council president for the borough of Manhattan. I had met Messenger a few months earlier at a meeting of the National League of Cities' Leadership Training Council. She was one of the people whose words and work convinced me that something new was afoot among practicing politicians, and that the city itself was teaching some of the more alert stewards of its accumulated power that the time had come for a more collaborative, more genuinely democratic way of engaging in the risk-taking entrepreneurship of that power.

Standing now in the presence of one of Messenger's risks, I remembered something she had said about the emerging form of political leadership. "Democracy is a system for turning the work of the community back to the community," she said, going on to call such democracy a system in which elected leaders act "not as visionaries but as facilitators, not as the people who provide all the answers, but as those who raise the right questions and identify new ways to encourage their communities to work together on finding the answers, moving citizens beyond the notion that they are simply taxpayers and service recipients to the notion that they must accept some responsibility to engage these issues with us if they want to find some real answers."

I knew all too well from my own political experience that the surliness of yesterday's election was a real force in the world, and that it must surely exist here among the produce booths at Union Square Market. But I knew from countless experiences in Missoula, in Santa Fe, and here in New York, that something very different was also afoot. Ruth Messenger was one of dozens of politicians who had taught me that lesson, and had taught me to look to the behavior of citizens to verify the lesson.

Heading home at last, I arrived at LaGuardia only to find that my flight had been cancelled. Knowing how much anger the innocent gate agent has to absorb in such a situation, I tried to keep my own weary annoyance within the bounds of civility. She quickly found me another flight on another airline, but it was due to depart in just a few minutes, from another terminal across the way. With no expectation of success, I dashed away, caught the bus, dashed again, and arrived at the other gate just as the last boarding call concluded.

As I entered the jetway, a voice from behind me called out breathlessly, "Mr. Kemmis?" Turning, I saw the gate agent from the cancelled flight running across the lobby toward me. "I forgot to give you your mileage credits for having to change airlines," she panted. I overcame my astonishment in time to tell her how appreciative I was; then I took the coupons she held out to me and made my final lunge to the safety of my westbound airplane. Settling into my seat at last, I said a silent goodbye to New York, grateful to have been taught once again, in the most unexpected way, what it might mean to become civilized.

Notes

1. THE GOOD LIFE

1. Christopher Alexander, *A New Theory of Urban Design* (New York: Oxford University Press, 1987), p. 2.

2. Ibid., p. 22.

3. Ibid., p. 22.

4. Tony Hiss, "Annals of Place (Baltimore)," *The New Yorker* April 29, 1991, 64.

5. Ibid., p. 65.

6. Ibid., p. 67.

7. Jane Jacobs, *The Death and Life of Great American Cities* (New York: Vintage Books, 1961), p. 432.

8. Ellen Posner, "A City That Likes Itself," *The Atlantic*, July 1991, 97.

9. Jane Jacobs, *The Death and Life of Great American Cities* (New York: Vintage Books, 1961), p. 434.

10. Ibid., p. 441.

2. A PLACE TO COME TOGETHER

1. Plutarch, *Selected Lives and Essays*, trans. Louise Ropes Loomis (Roslyn, New York: Walter Jay Black, Inc., 1951), pp. 12–13.

2. Jane Jacobs, *The Death and Life of Great American Cities* (New York: Vintage Books, 1961), p. 82. Emphasis in the original.

3. Plutarch, *Selected Lives and Essays*, trans. Louise Ropes Loomis (Roslyn, New York: Walter Jay Black, Inc., 1951), p. 12.

3. THE CHARACTER OF THE CITY

1. James Hillman, "Talking as Walking," in *Stirrings of Culture: Essays from the Dallas Institute,* ed. Robert Sardello and Gail Thomas (Dallas: Dallas Institute Publications, 1986), p. 13.
2. Ibid., p. 12.
3. Cited in "Searching for the Soul of Dallas," by Mark Gauvreau Judge in *Common Boundary* 10, no. 6 (November 1992): 47.
4. Virgil, *The Aeneid,* trans. Robert Fitzgerald (New York: Vintage Books, 1981), p. 19.
5. Lewis Mumford, *The City in History* (San Diego, New York, London: Harvest/HBJ, 1956), p. 140.
6. Ibid.

4. THE HEALTH OF CITIES

1. Aristotle, *Politics,* ed. and trans. Ernest Barker (New York: Oxford University Press, 1962), p. 6.
2. Tyler Norris, *Healthy Communities Handbook* (Denver: The National Civic League, 1993), p. 6.

5. FOCUSING THE COUNTRYSIDE

1. Neal R. Peirce, *Citistates* (Washington, D.C.: Seven Locks Press, 1993), p. 1.
2. Ibid., p. x.
3. Jane Jacobs, *Cities and the Wealth of Nations* (New York: Vintage Books, 1984), p. 200.
4. Neal R. Peirce, *Citistates* (Washington, D.C.: Seven Locks Press, 1993), p. 12.
5. David Rusk, "The Metropolitan Perplex: Suburban Renewal," *Nation's Cities Weekly,* November 8, 1993, 4.
6. Ibid.

6. A SISTERHOOD OF CITY-STATES

1. Martin Heidegger, "Building, Dwelling, Thinking," in *Poetry, Language, Thought,* trans. Albert Hofstadter (New York: Harper & Row, 1975), p. 150.

7. THE GOOD POLITICIAN

1. Michael Sandel, "The Procedural Republic, and the Unencumbered Self," *Political Theory* 12 (February 1984):81–96.
2. Machiavelli, *The Prince,* trans. W. K. Marriot (New York: E. P. Dutton & Co., 1916), pp. 205–206.
3. Ibid., p. 181.
4. Christopher Alexander, *A New Theory of Urban Design* (New York: Oxford University Press, 1987), p. 2.
5. Martin Heidegger, "Building, Dwelling, Thinking," in *Poetry, Language, Thought,* trans. Albert Hofstadter (New York: Harper & Row, 1975), pp. 152, 154.
6. Rumi, *Open Secret: Versions of Rumi,* trans. John Moyne and Coleman Barks (Putney, Vt.: Threshold Books, 1984), p. 17.

8. THE GOOD CITIZEN

1. Ed Fouhy, "The Dawn of Public Journalism," *National Civic Review* 83, no. 3 (summer 1994): 260.
2. Ibid., 264.
3. Martin Heidegger, "Building, Dwelling, Thinking," in *Poetry, Language, Thought,* trans. Albert Hofstadter (New York: Harper & Row, 1975), pp. 152–153.

Index